MAZE OF JUSTICE
Diary of a Country Prosecutor

MAZE OF JUSTICE

Diary of a Country Prosecutor

an Egyptian novel
by Tawfik al-Hakim
translated by Abba Eban
Foreword by P.H. Newby

Saqi Books

British Library Cataloguing in Publication Data

Hakim, Tawfiq, *1898–1987*
 Maze of Justice.
 1. Arabic literature. Egyptian writers. Hakim Tawfiq
 – Critical studies
 I. Title II. Yawmiyyat na'eb fil aryaf. *English*
 892.'78509

 ISBN 0–86356–200–0

First published in 1947 by
The Harvill Press, London

This edition first published in 1989 by
Saqi Books, 26 Westbourne Grove, London W2
© 1947 Tawfik al-Hakim; © 1989 Zeinab al-Hakim;
Foreword © 1989 P.H. Newby

Printed in Great Britain.

Typeset in 11 point Bembo by Theatretexts, London

Foreword

Readers usually skip an introduction, but in spite of this I must say one or two things that may help in the appreciation of this novel by one of the leading contributors to modern Arabic literature. *Maze of Justice* purports to be the diary of a Public Prosecutor stationed about sixty years ago in a small town somewhere in the Egyptian Delta. You would have discovered this for yourself. Not only that, you would have seen that, in spite of the misery and poverty by which he is surrounded, the Public Prosecutor has a strong sense of humour and a sharp eye for the absurd. These are Egyptian characteristics.

But there are other points to be made. Tawfik al-Hakim's comedy is blacker than anything Gogol or Dickens wrote because life for the Egyptian peasantry, the fellahin, was blacker than for the nineteenth-century Russian serf or English pauper. It must also be said that the first readers of Gogol and Dickens would not have been prepared to look at unwelcome facts with the honesty Tawfik al-Hakim expected of his readers. The Egyptian reading public all those years ago (the novel was first published in 1937) was, in its cynical way, more realistic than the reading public in Tsarist Russia or Victorian England. The savage satire of the book is, as a result — and by general consent — on target.

The title of the English translation is a bit misleading because it implies a Kafka-like complexity of administration with the possibility that the centre of the maze can be reached and justice done. The reality is different. The theme of the book is that justice is of no importance at all to the powers-that-be. All that matters is the paperwork which, provided it meets bureaucratic

requirements, is accepted, classified and filed away without regard to right and wrong. Justice is certainly of no concern to the judge who regularly comes up from Cairo. What really concerns him is buying the best local meat and catching the 11 a.m. train home again, no matter how many cases have to be rushed through without considering the evidence. There are other astonishing abuses. A wretch on the point of death from poisoning is questioned mercilessly so that the appropriate form can be filled in, with date of birth, state of the victim's health before the poisoning, symptoms and the *exact* time when they first appeared. Again, a man known by the police to be innocent is wrongly picked out on an identity parade and taken into custody because that is the official routine. And so on.

The helpless victims of this tyranny are bewildered country folk. Their immediate oppressors are the local bosses (the chief of police, the ma'mur, and other office-holders) but especially the legal system itself. It was foreign, based on the Code Napoléon, and took such little account of local conditions that peasants could not understand what they had done wrong. To them it seemed right and proper for a starving man to feed himself and his family with wheat he had grown himself; but it had been 'reserved' by the court until he paid tax on it. The fact that he had eaten something of which he was supposed to be a trustee was a crime for which he gets one month with hard labour. 'Do you hear me, Muslims! My own wheat! My own crop! My own property!'

The fellah is a peaceable not to say submissive figure, as likely as not, sixty years ago, to be suffering from one or perhaps two of the country's enfeebling diseases. If it so happens that he wants to kill somebody, he scrapes together enough money to hire one of the professional killers, nearly all foreigners, 'bedu from the Sudan', who are less squeamish than himself. Stubborn he can be but defiance is alien to his nature, so he comes to believe that the law is administered by madmen and goes back helplessly to his plot of beans or maize. But the law is not administered by madmen; they are just despairing and cynical bureaucrats who regard the real power in the state as foreign and therefore arbitrary and unpredictable.

Throughout the centuries, the real rulers of Egypt had been foreigners, most recently Mamelukes, Turks and then the dynasty

founded by the Albanian Muhammad Ali early in the nineteenth century. On the whole they were remote from the native Egyptians, whose response was, as it had been from time immemorial, to keep their heads down. When in 1882 the British came nothing was changed for the fellahin because the British were not interested in land reform. The fellah's 'madman' was merely an Egyptian official who believed that the big questions of power and destiny were insoluble and all he could do was look after his own interests as best he could. Politics was a game played for personal advantage (when was it not?) but the difference in Egypt was that there was no embarrassment about corruption. It was the order of nature. So when an election came along the ma'mur could with a good conscience tip the ballot box into the river and replace it with a box containing the votes he had prepared himself. Even the Public Prosecutor of *Maze of Justice*, sensitive and liberal as he is, succumbs to the system of which he is a part.

The savage humour is what chiefly drives the narrative along but another element is the macabre fun that turns up here and there. It seems very Egyptian and, more specifically, very Cairene. Jokes about the casual taking of human life appear in some of those tales from *The Thousand and One Nights* that are thought to have been written in Cairo. In *Maze of Justice* there is a spirited scene where the town barber, under the supervision of the Public Prosecutor and a pathologist, drags corpse after corpse out of first one grave and then another in a muddled attempt to locate the body of a woman who has been murdered. The comedy is grim but comedy it is. On another occasion the Public Prosecutor reflects that 'human life has no value in Egypt' and, visiting the Government Hospital where swarms of women in their black clothes and blue amulets stand shouting and sobbing, records that, 'Then I knew that [the sentry] would soon fling a corpse to them; for every day a corpse or two would be thrown outside these walls, an offering to the grief that lay waiting by the gate.' This was al-Hakim's way of saying patients had died and would be handed over to the relatives.

Tawfik al-Hakim (1898-1987) had been a Public Prosecutor in the Delta himself and wrote out of first-hand experience. It has been said that *Maze of Justice* is a detective story. True, there is a murder and an investigation but the reader's expectations would

be aroused in quite the wrong way if he thought he was in for a whodunnit. He would become impatient of the incompetent way the investigation is carried out and its failure to name the culprit. It is not that sort of novel at all. It is about man's inhumanity to man and the murder investigation is just a way of tying the different elements of the diary together.

For the educated lawyer like the Public Prosecutor (and perhaps for Tawfik al-Hakim himself) the fellahin have a certain mystery. Surely their lives cannot be as wretched as they seem? One character in the story, the eccentric Shaikh Asfur, represents something about the Delta and its inhabitants that remains elusive. He sings cryptic snatches of song instead of answering questions, he appears to know more about what is going on than anyone in authority and yet he keeps his mouth shut either out of perversity or for some other more obscure motive. If this were really a detective story he would be one of the suspects. He is a free spirit when everyone else, fellahin and the local worthies, are prisoners of circumstance. Another elusive person is the girl Rim, so beautiful that jaws drop at the sight of her. By her very appearance she contradicts the world she lives in; and yet again, if this were a whodunnit she would be a suspect because she had motive enough to hire one of the professional murderers. She says and does very little but is a real presence in the story.

So, too, is the Delta itself: hot, dusty, boring in its flatness, where the mind has to be distracted by endless cups of coffee and catnaps. The stillness of the night is boring too, broken only by the sound of animals and perhaps a remote pumping machine. Boring, that is to say, to the young bloods of the place who yearn for Cairo, the bright lights, the cabarets, the excitement, just as provincials in nineteenth-century Russia yearned for Moscow. Tawfik al-Hakim's bitter humour focused on a social reality that he plainly regarded as shocking and, since he saw no immediate way of improving it, dispiriting.

P.H. Newby

P.H. NEWBY lived for several years in Egypt and taught at Gizeh University, then known as Fouad al-Awal University. Zagazig was one of the places in the Delta he used to visit regularly and

he suspects this cannot be far from the setting of *Maze of Justice*. His first novel, *A Journey to the Interior* (1945), was followed by many others, notably *The Picnic at Sakkara* and *Something to Answer For*, both of which are set in Egypt. He was awarded the Somerset Maugham Prize in 1948 and the Booker Prize in 1969.

His interest in and affection for Egypt have never faltered and he has published, with the American photographer Fred Maroon, *The Egypt Story* (1979) and a study of ancient Egypt, *Warrior Pharaohs* (1980). A biography, *Saladin in his Time*, was published in 1983.

For further reading

al-Hakim, Tewfik, *The Tree Climber*, trans. Denys Johnson-Davies (London, 1966)
—— *Fate of a Cockroach: Four Plays of Freedom*, trans. Denys Johnson-Davies (London, 1973)
—— *Plays, Prefaces and Postscripts of Tawfik al-Hakim* (two vols), trans. William M. Hutchins (Washington, DC, 1981 and 1984)
Hourani, Albert, *Arabic Thought in the Liberal Age* (London, 1962)
Manzalaoui, Mahmoud (ed.), *Arabic Writing Today: Drama* (Cairo, 1977)

Glossary

bedu	nomad, desert-dweller
effendi	title of respect
Fatiha	opening verse of the Quran
fellahin	peasants
galabieh	simple cotton robe worn by fellahin
ghafir	watchman or sentry
Haj	literally, one who has been on the pilgrimage to Mecca; but often a term of respect for an old man
howdah	a canopied seat on the back of a camel or an elephant
ma'mur	administrative officer in charge of a district, responsible for police and security matters
nargilah	oriental pipe or hubble-bubble
qadi	religious (Islamic) judge
Ramadan	the Muslim month of fasting
Shaikh	courtesy title given to old people (literally, one who can recite the whole Quran)
Sirat	the bridge, narrower than a hair and sharper than a sword, which, according to Muslim tradition, all men must cross on the Day of Judgement
umdah	head of a village

A Note on Tawfik al-Hakim

Tawfik al-Hakim was born in Alexandria in 1898. He went to Paris to study law and came under the spell of European theatre. After returning to Egypt he published his first novel, *The Return of the Spirit* (1933), which captured the Arab mood of national awakening and won its author immediate acclaim. He worked for a time as a Public Prosecutor in a small provincial town, an experience put to good use in his second novel, *Maze of Justice* (1937), which was partly autobiographical.

Al-Hakim was a prolific writer, producing several volumes of short stories and essays, as well as two other novels and a memoir. But he is perhaps best known as the father of the modern Arab theatre. His many plays deal with philosophical and religious issues, often intertwining Christian and Islamic themes, and exploring social questions such as the position of women, the individual's quest for freedom within society, and the pursuit of happiness in a world scarred by war, disease and poverty. For Arab audiences of the time, these were strikingly modern and cosmopolitan themes. In technique, too, al-Hakim was an innovator in a medium which had only recently struck root in Arab culture. Experimental plays such as *The Tree Climber* (1962) — a product of the Theatre of the Absurd — were radically new, and al-Hakim's treatment of language, dialogue and form influenced a generation of Arab dramatists.

Al-Hakim's modernism was that of the Westernized liberal intellectual. Like other influential figures of his time, such as the blind Egyptian writer and educational reformer Taha Hussein, he was an enthusiastic admirer of European civilization. The limits of liberal idealism, apparent to a later generation, were much less obvious to Arab intellectuals of the 1930s and 1940s. Al-Hakim and Hussein and many of their contemporaries believed Europe's colonial yoke had to be thrown off, but this did not shake their faith in its arts and sciences, its political institutions, and above all the national ideal which it embodied.

Maze of Justice, while universal in its appeal as a social comedy, is a product of this formative period in Egypt's development. It was an era which Tawfik al-Hakim outlived, becoming an elder statesman of Arabic letters. Yet he remained, until his death in July 1987, one of its foremost exemplars.

Roger Hardy

…Why am I thus disposed to set down the daily record of my life? Certainly not because my life is happy. He that lives a happy life does not record it; he is content to live it. I spend my days enmeshed in the coils of human frailty. It is my close companion, the consort on whose face I gaze each day, never being able to commune with her alone. Here in this diary I may speak freely of her and of myself, and of all that breathes on earth. These pages, doomed never to see the light of publication, are an open window wherefrom I send my thoughts roaming free in hours of anguish.

11 October

I went to bed early last night. I had an inflamed throat —
an affliction which comes upon me quite often these days.
I tied a woollen rag round my neck, baited the three mouse-
traps with bits of ancient cheese and laid them round my
bed, as one lays protective mines around a hospital ship. I
put out the paraffin lamp and closed my eyes — praying that
God might cause erring human instincts to rest awhile within
the district, so that no crime should compel me to get up
while I was feeling indisposed. I laid my head upon the
pillow and was soon sleeping like a log.

I was awakened by the sound of the ghafir knocking
violently on the door and shouting to my servant, 'Wake
up, Dessouki!' I then realized that a crime had been
committed. Erring human instincts had not slept in deference
to my need of sleep. I got up without delay and lit the oil
lamp. My servant came in, rubbing his eyes with one hand
and holding out a telephone message with the other. I held
the paper near the light and read, 'Tonight at 8 p.m. while
Kamar al-Dawla Alwan was walking on the river-side, near
our village, a shot was fired at him from a sugar-plantation
by a person or persons unknown. On being interrogated the

victim was unable to divulge anything. His condition is grave. For your information. The Umdah.'

'That's all right,' I thought to myself — 'a simple matter. It won't take me more than a couple of hours at the most. The assailant is unknown. The victim cannot speak and won't confuse me with his chatter. I have no doubt what the witnesses will be like. There will be the ghafir on duty who heard the shot, went off towards it, sluggish with fright — and naturally found nothing but a body prostrate on the ground. Then there will be the umdah, who will swear by his wife's honour that the criminal is not one of his villagers; and, finally, the members of the victim's family, who will keep everything dark from me and reserve the opportunities of vengeance for themselves.'

I asked my servant the time, and wrote it down at the bottom of the message: 'Received 10 p.m. Proceeding to investigate.'

I rushed to my clothes, dressed with frantic speed, like a member of a fire-brigade, and sent for my clerk and official car. I then dispatched a messenger to awaken my new assistant, a mild-mannered fellow, recently appointed, who had implored me to take him along on these investigations, so that he might gain experience and practice.

A few minutes passed, and then I heard the horn of the office Ford blowing outside my gate. Seated in it were the ma'mur, the inspector and a few policemen. I went down to join them, and found everything ready — except the clerk. This did not surprise me as I had never been late for any case, in any village or district, without the clerk being responsible for my delay. I turned to the ghafir and asked, 'Are you certain that you called Said Effendi?'

In the thick gloom I heard the sound of a heavy boot stamping on the ground, saw a hand being raised in military salute above the long felt cap with the bronze badge, and observed a mouth moving under a huge black moustache like a cat's tail: 'He put his shirt on in my presence, sir.'

We decided to go off in our car and pick up the clerk at his house on the way. I drove with my assistant and the ma'mur in the departmental car until we reached a fairly new house on the outskirts of the village. The ghafir, who was hanging on to our running-board and acting as our guide, shouted, 'Come down, Said Effendi.'

The clerk, still in his nightshirt, looked out of a distant window: 'Is there a case?'

'A shooting case,' yelled the ghafir.

I noticed the ma'mur's fist emerging from the window of the car and descending vigorously on the back of the ghafir's neck: 'Wretched fellow — so he put his shirt on in your presence, did he, you...!'

'On my word of honour, sir — he *had* put it on, I assure you...'

I saw no point in holding an inquiry into this matter, as there were only two possibilities — either the ghafir did not know the difference between a shirt and a nightshirt, which would not have been surprising; or else Said Effendi had taken his shirt off again and gone back to sleep — which would not have surprised me either. In any case, since I was the only one officially responsible for the delay, there was nothing to be gained by an argument with Said Effendi except a splitting headache; and I needed rest more than anyone that night, as I had to reserve my energy and power of speech for the actual case which was causing all this trouble. Languor crept over my limbs. I rested my head against the corner of the car, remarking to my companion, 'The scene of the crime is thirty kilometres away. There's no harm in my dozing during the journey.'

I closed my eyes. Our car moved off, followed by the Ford van, containing the clerk, the inspector, the police corporal and the constables. Almost as soon as we came out on the country road, we heard a voice singing in the darkness of the night. The ma'mur instantly put his head out of the window and shouted, 'Inspector — we've forgotten Shaikh Asfur.'

17

The convoy halted. A voice was heard rising clearly from a thicket at the edge of a field:

> My loved one's eyelash, long and dark,
> Would span an acre wide.

Out he came — that strange creature who wanders aimlessly by night and day, a sleepless vagrant eternally humming the same songs, mouthing stray words, uttering predictions which win the credence of simple folk. Nothing gives the man more pleasure than to go out on investigations with the Legal Officer and the police. Whenever he hears the horn of the Ford van blowing in the distance he follows it wheresoever it goes, like a dog following its master to the chase. What does it all mean? For a long time I have been asking myself whether this fellow may not be the possessor of some strange secret.

He approached the Ford and said, rather querulously, 'You were going off without me?'

The police corporal answered with a smile, 'If we'd known your address, we would have sent a message.'

'Very well,' he replied, 'give me a cigarette.'

The corporal winked at him quickly and said in a low voice, 'Shut up — the ma'mur will hear you!'

'Give me a cigarette,' persisted Shaikh Asfur. 'Come on, corporal — I'm a corporal, too, tonight — in the smokeless army.'

He got into the Ford van with the air of a man entering a Rolls Royce, first plucking a twig from a thicket and carrying it as though it were a royal sceptre.

The two vehicles drove on between the maize plantations. Nature slept and all voices were stilled, save for the croaking of frogs and the chirp of crickets, and the melodious sound of Shaikh Asfur's voice coming from the interior of the Ford.

I had lapsed into the drowsy torpor which usually came

upon me while driving to an investigation — only a partial torpor which did not prevent me from catching an occasional sentence of the conversation going on around me. My assistant sat on my left, wide awake, eager curiosity written all over his face. It was clear that he was bursting to ask me all sorts of questions and was only restrained by the fear of disturbing and irritating me. So he turned to the ma'mur sitting close to him and they were soon caught up in a long conversation, of which very little penetrated my consciousness. Their chatter plunged me into deep slumber the whole way and I only awoke when the car stopped after a fairly long interval. I opened my eyes and saw that we had a canal in front of us, and that the ferry-boat was waiting to take us over to the other bank. We got out of our car and crowded into the boat like marooned seamen in a life-saving dinghy, or earthen pots piled up in a Nile barge. The ferry took us across to the further bank.

No sound disturbed the deep silence of the night except the chains of the ferry-boat clanging in the water. Nothing was to be seen in the thick darkness. As soon as we touched land, we heard the whinnying of horses, and saw the police station's mounts and the umdah's donkeys drawn up before us ready to convey us to the scene of the crime. Some horses they were, too! One of the policemen came towards me with a restive beast, in deference to my rank and position. I saw how it snorted and stamped the ground with its hooves, scarcely patient enough to wait for me to mount it. I realized that I was absolutely doomed to be thrown. I had very often come near to toppling off the backs of those sportive steeds, which need an experienced horseman to master them — not a rider half asleep with exhaustion. How I would have preferred a nice quiet donkey! I looked around furtively and saw the notables of our party already in their saddles, leaving the donkeys for the less exalted crowd. I was ashamed to dismount from my horse and put myself on the same level as Shaikh Asfur, who had seated himself on a grey donkey,

smacked it with his green sceptre and moved off in the rear of the column.

I commended my soul to the Almighty and rode forward at the head of the party, reeling with fright and exhaustion. At length sleep came over my eyelids and all was oblivion — until I suddenly became aware of my body flying off the horse's back and coming to rest around its neck. The animal had jumped so violently into a canal that the impact had wrenched me off its back. 'Just as I feared,' I thought to myself. I shouted to the ghafir in charge of my mount, 'The horse, man, the horse!'

The party stopped in disarray. The ma'mur lavishly distributed words of abuse, slaps, commands and prohibitions to his faithful followers until they finally restored me to the back of my horse, where I tried to hide my shame, saying, 'The horse must have fallen asleep while walking, or been frightened by a running fox and startled. Anyway — keep hold of the bridle, ghafir.'

Two ghafirs did my bidding and led me along slowly, with a peaceful measured gait, which sent me back to sleep again.

I awoke at the scene of the crime, where I saw the light of lamps and torches in the hands of the crowd gathered round the victim. My fatigue flew away like an owl flying from its nest at the approach of dawn. I dismounted briskly and cleaved a way through the crowd, which greeted me with a low murmur: 'Here comes the Legal Officer.' I drew near the body lying prostrate on the ground and scrutinized the face, which was befouled with soil and blood. It was quite clear to me that he would certainly not be able to speak.

I found the officer in charge of the police station up to his ears in the compilation of a 'statement' for me to throw into the waste-paper basket. For the Legal Officer always investigates the case anew as soon as he arrives. We settled down to the inquiry, beginning with the description of our arrival. The clerk took his pen and paper, came to my side

and wrote, while I dictated the usual formula:

'We, the Legal Officer and district clerk at o'clock received a telephone message, number to the effect that, etc, etc. We proceeded by car to the region of where we arrived at such-and-such an hour, whereupon the present Situation Report begins, etc, etc.'

The point is that I always like to take pains with the compilation of the Report and to see that it is well and logically arranged. The Report is the be-all-and-end-all in the eyes of higher authority. It is the only evidence testifying to the accuracy and skill of the Legal Officer. Nobody worries, of course, about the mere apprehension of the criminal.

The preamble was followed by a description of the assault, the clothes worn by the victim and the place in which he was found. We saw no reason to be brief. I dictated to the clerk a detailed description of the ugly red wound whose widening fissure we had seen in the victim's shoulder. It seemed to me to have been caused by small-arms fire from a fairly short distance, tearing the flesh and causing haemorrhage. We described the victim's face very fully. It was that of a man about forty, of handsome, distinguished appearance — a typically provincial sort of distinction marked by robust virility and strength. We did not forget to mention the likeness of the bird tattooed on his upper temple or the colour of his moustache veering towards yellow. We enumerated all the articles of his clothing, from the overcoat, the galabieh of spun cotton and the untouched money-wallet, down to the white linen drawers with the red cord. Yes — we did not even leave out the red cord and the way it was spun. Mention of small details indicates accuracy and vigilance. That is the tradition of investigation which we had all inherited from our superiors. I remember that I once left a wounded man in the throes of death-agony and began to describe his trousers, sandals and cap until, when I had finished and leaned over the victim to ask who

21

had attacked him, I found that he had expired.

Nor did we omit to describe the place of the crime — a narrow path between two fields of sugar-cane. This was not surprising. Every kind of plantation produces its harvest of crime. With the sprouting of the maize and sugar-cane comes the season of murder by shooting. As the wheat and barley turn yellow, autumn comes, with its crop of arson and incendiarism, and when the cotton turns green we get an increase in the uprooting and destruction of trees and plants.

We had finished with the dying victim, who no longer concerned us, now that we had crammed our Report full with his particulars; so we left him wallowing in his blood, under the care of the station police officer, until such time as the ambulance men would come to take him off to hospital. We went off to the umdah's 'saloon', where coffee awaited us.

I know all there is to be known about umdahs' coffee. I always call it 'chloroform', for it has never failed to have on me the opposite effect from that which it is meant to produce. I don't know why it is; but I did notice one night that a certain umdah called his servant — in our hearing — to bring 'bean coffee'. At the time I could not understand the point of adding the word 'bean' to the 'coffee'. Was it merely a tautology for the sake of emphasis, or a token of honour and respect for the guest? I cannot say. All I did learn with complete certainty that night was that the 'bean' — whatever it was doing in the composition of the sentence — played no part at all in the composition of the coffee.

We sat in the 'reception room' on a sofa of velvet which had long since lost its hair and colour. The clerk arranged his papers on a limping stool, surmounted by a layer of broken marble, and then spread out his Report in the light of a lamp with a resounding sizzle, which had attracted the nocturnal mosquitoes in their scores. I called for the witnesses. The ma'mur took up the call, and shouted, 'Assemble the witnesses, please, inspector.'

He then threw himself down into an easy chair in the

corner of the room in an attitude which left no doubt in my mind that nothing was to be expected of him thenceforth but sleep, interspersed with snoring. My assistant sat by me watching the proceedings with apathetic eyes, for languor had beguiled him as the zephyr breeze beguiles leaves on a tree.

First they brought the duty-ghafir, who had heard the shot and been the first to rush to the scene of the crime. He did not fail to live up to my expectations — except in one thing. He insisted that he had heard two shots, whereas the text of the message referred to one shot; and the wound was caused by one shot only. All the villagers agreed that no more than one shot had rung out that evening. What motive could he have for lying? I was completely baffled. So we put aside the more important aspects of the case and went off into a discussion of the question whether one or two shots were fired. We interrogated everybody anew, and their answers were of one accord: 'One shot, sir!'

'And you, the ghafir, heard — how many shots?'

'Two, sir.'

'Are you certain?'

'Two shots, sir.'

I was left to reflect on the wearisome slowness of investigation and the incalculable irritations of this job. I could understand an accused man lying — that is part of his natural right and I should never expect him to tell me the truth. But a witness — for heaven's sake, what can induce him to cast a veil of equivocation and contradiction over the naked truth?

The investigation wound its way through obscure paths, illumined by no hope of reaching any tangible result. Nobody knew who the assailant might be. Nobody suspected anyone. The victim had no family in the village except an old sick mother, whose sight had failed and who had lost the faculty of speech. His wife had died two years previously, leaving a child, too young for us to interrogate. Nobody could

suggest a reasonable or unreasonable motive for the assault. Nobody knew of any enmity between the victim and any living person which might have led to the commission of the crime. Had some demon arisen from murky hell and shot the man dead? Nobody knew anything.

It was, in fact, precisely as I had expected. From the moment I had read the telephone message for the first time I had realized that the case was 'dead'. Could I with my process of 'investigation' hope to breathe life into a lifeless thing? If the witnesses were not going to come forward with the truth and the villagers were not going to help me willingly and sincerely — how could any 'Report' ever written obtain for me the honoured privilege of looking at a real live felon face to face?

The umdah came forward to testify in his turn. He took the oath and we began to ply him with the same useless questions. Suddenly a snore arose from the corner of the room and drowned the inquiry. I turned round — and there was the ma'mur asleep, his chin on his hand, leaning against the canopy. The umdah observed my gesture and, asking my leave, went off towards the ma'mur and woke him up gently: 'Excuse me, sir, there is a bed in the other room.'

He conducted him with quiet courtesy to an adjoining room in the back of the house; and then returned to recite to me the official hackneyed utterances which bore the unmistakable stamp of his position. The words and phrases are of a type — they scarcely vary at all between one umdah and another. In any case, they do neither good nor harm, and blow a cool refreshing breeze over the flaming cauldron of crime.

The umdah appended to his statement a signature rather like the track of a chicken's claw on the ground. He had barely left the place where the witnesses had been giving their evidence when the door of the back room opened and the ma'mur appeared, scratching himself vigorously, picking things out of his clothes and flicking them away. He was

foaming with rage and grumbling violently. 'What a bed! My God — what use are you as an umdah?!'

I understood what had happened and laughed inwardly, giving the appearance of intense absorption in my work and keeping my face glued to the documents before me. The ma'mur resumed his seat with the air of one who had renounced all thought of further sleep that night and briskly addressed the umdah: 'Anyway — bring some coffee; and, for heaven's sake, see that it's made properly.'

He then turned to me and spoke as if he were trying to keep the evening lively: 'Case proceeding satisfactorily, I hope?'

The object of this expression was to elicit how the case was going and what chance we had of success. ('Success' meant that somebody's head would be forfeit on the gallows.)

I replied in a low murmur without looking up, 'The case is fast asleep.'

Suddenly the ma'mur sprang to his feet as though he had suddenly remembered the key to the whole enigma: 'Shaikh Asfur!'

The mysterious fellow's head emerged from behind a wicker chair in a dark corner of the room. He drew himself up formally with his green sceptre as though he were being presented at Court.

'What is your opinion, Shaikh Asfur?'

I could stand no more. That was all we needed — the advice of crazy lunatics in murder cases! I gave the ma'mur a significant look. He drew closer: 'Shaikh Asfur is an absolute gem. Once he led us to a suspect's shotgun buried in the canal.'

'My dear ma'mur, instead of questioning Shaikh Asfur or Shaikh Tartur, or whatever he calls himself, kindly take the trouble to go along with the inspector and his men and search the houses of all possible suspects in the village.'

The inspector came in from where he had been waiting outside the room. He had heard my orders to the ma'mur

and handed his chief a paper headed, Report on Search (One Page): 'We have carried out the search already, sir.'

The ma'mur handed it to me without looking at it. I glanced swiftly through the verbose, expansive text until I finally came to the familiar sentence: 'We discovered no arms or forbidden articles of any sort or kind.'

I scribbled at the bottom of the page, 'To be filed with Report' and clasped my head in my hands, wondering what was to be done next in this case, and whom we could interrogate so as to bring our Report up to a minimum of twenty pages. For I have never forgotten what a Public Prosecutor said to me one day when he received a ten-page Report: 'What's all this? A contravention or a misdemeanour?'

When I replied that it was a murder case, he shouted at me in astonishment, 'A murder case investigated in ten pages! An assassination! The murder of a human being! All in ten pages?'

When I replied that with those ten pages we had managed to get the murderer, he paid no attention whatever and went on weighing the Report in his hand with careful accuracy: 'Who would ever have believed that this Report could be of a murder case?'

I replied instantly, 'Next time, God willing, we shall be more careful about the weight!'

That incident recurred to my mind as I sat silent and downcast... My reflections were interrupted by the voice of the crazy Shaikh raised in song, which reverberated through the room:

Watch out for women; they're the mark
Of ruin to men's pride;
My loved one's eyelash, long and dark,
Would span an acre wide!

I was not angry with the Shaikh for violating the dignity

26

of the law with his tuneful jingle and I did not chase him out of the room. I pondered for a moment on the meaning of his rhyme — insofar as it had any coherent meaning. The only noteworthy point was his reference to women.

His advice was to look for women suspects, not men. Which women? I had never come across a case more innocent of female interest than this. The victim had been living alone since the death of his wife. There was nobody on close terms with him except his old infirm mother, who could scarcely be regarded as a dangerous 'mystery woman'. Well, it was obvious that Asfur did not know what he was talking about. He was just an old shaikh in a green turban repeating words and songs like a parrot, without meaning anything by them. But wait a minute! The victim had a small child. Could it possibly be in the charge of his old bedridden mother?

'One moment — umdah.'

I put the question to him. He replied with childlike innocence and complete simplicity, 'The child is in the care of the young girl.'

'What girl?'

'You know — the girl. The sister of his dead wife.'

'Grown up?'

'Yes — a young lady.'

I turned to the inspector and asked him to bring the girl at once.

She soon appeared — a young girl of sixteen. Never since my arrival in the provinces had I seen a more lovely face or a more graceful figure. She stood in the doorway clad in a long black robe like an ebony statue engraved with a white countenance. The umdah spoke to her encouragingly: 'Come in, young lady.'

She advanced shyly with hesitant steps, not knowing before whom to stand. The umdah directed her towards me. She looked me straight in the face, raising her eyelids. For the first time in my experience I knew what it was to be ill at ease during an investigation. I could think of no question

to ask her. The clerk could not see her as she was standing behind him. So when he noticed my silence, he assumed that I was tired. He dipped his pen in the ink, raised his eyes and asked, 'Your name?'

Having fixed his eyes on her, he remained staring and gave no heed to his papers. I looked round and saw that my drowsy assistant had been quickened to sudden energy and had begun to stare at the girl open-eyed. I transferred my gaze to the ma'mur and found him in no need of coffee, with or without beans. Shaikh Asfur had crept up to my feet and was now crouching like a dog, staring up at the beautiful peasant girl with gaping mouth. Beauty is certainly an awe-inspiring force. I decided that the moment had come to pull myself together before my troubled state became too apparent. I lowered my gaze so as not to see her beauty and said, 'Your name?'

'Rim.'

She pronounced the name non-committally. My whole being vibrated like a violin chord to the touch of deft and sensitive fingers. I felt certain that my voice would tremble if I asked her anything else, so I hesitated. The position was distinctly embarrassing, for the investigation would drag on interminably if I was going to halt blankly between each question. I collected my scattered wits, and all the resolution I could muster, and charged into the breach with questions framed to elicit a long complete answer: 'Tell me all about it, please.'

I waited, my eyes fixed upon her. And then I realized with deep astonishment what the position was. Up to that moment she did not know what had happened to the victim. She had just been awakened and brought before me without being told anything. I did not want to tell her of it yet awhile, for there was something going on inside her which I could only grasp intuitively.

I asked if anyone had asked her hand in marriage. She answered affirmatively. The last suitor had been a nice young

28

man whom she would not have rejected; but her brother-in-law, who was her guardian, had rejected him. He had always refused to accept any of the numerous men whose hands had been outstretched towards her like the hands of praying votaries.

'Have you a grudge against anyone because of this?'

'No.' She pronounced the denial with an intensity which struck me as unusual.

'Had you anything to do with the young man?'

She admitted that she had. There had been two innocent meetings in front of her house, when he had learnt from her that she did not object to him as a husband but was reluctant to disobey her guardian. What could her guardian's motive be in rejecting all suitors? Was it excessive zeal in the girl's interest? Was it because he thought this particular match inadequate for her? She did not know what hidden motive he might have. She was very eager to know it. What was against it? Nothing, as far as she could see. She simply could not explain it. Solution of riddles is a gift not granted to all: and the power to solve them requires an accurate knowledge of motives lying concealed in the deepest recesses of men's hearts. This girl, as it seemed to me, had a mind like a thicket of reeds and sugar-cane, whose dark foundations saw no light except in fragments, like dancing coins, flashing in the dark, whenever the reeds inclined this way or that...

'Have the ambulance people turned up to take the wounded man away?'

'Yes — a long time ago.'

Realization dawned on the girl and a scream burst from her mouth, which she hastily smothered in deference to us. I was sure that its echoes reverberated in her inmost heart. I tried to go on with my inquiry but now I had before me a girl whose disjointed speech had no coherence or usefulness at all.

I decided to postpone the investigation. 'Sit down and rest, Rim,' I said.

29

I turned to the ma'mur: 'We had better finish the investigation in the morning.'

He pointed to the window. Daylight was already stealing in but the light of the lamp had prevented me from noticing it. I sprang to my feet, suddenly remembering that the criminal court was in session that day and I had omitted to arrange overnight for one of my colleagues to deputize for me. There was nothing for it but to return with all speed so as to be in time for the session.

'Inspector, bring the girl in the van.'

We suspended our summary of evidence and arranged to resume the investigation in the Legal Department Office after the session of the court. We mounted our animals and rode back, Shaikh Asfur bringing up the rear, brandishing his green stick like a warrior in the agitation of the fray, and shouting, 'She's the one!'

'Keep quiet,' retorted the ma'mur.

'She's the one — she with those eyelashes — I know her — those eyelashes of hers!'

'Shut up, Shaikh Asfur. You'd better watch out or you'll fall off that donkey of yours!'

Fatigue crept over my limbs and I drooped in the saddle; but the fresh morning breeze kept caressing my face with gentle strokes, like the waving of a fan in the hands of a lovely maid. This prevented me from losing my alertness and I became plunged in deep reflection. Suddenly Asfur's song burst out violently as though something had exploded within his very heart:

> My loved one's eyelash, long and dark...
> Would span...

I did not hear the rest of the verse; what I heard was something falling to the ground. We turned and found Shaikh Asfur in his shabby robes 'spanning' a good piece of earth. We halted. The ghafir hurried to his aid and put him back

on his donkey. He sat bolt upright, brushed the dirt off himself and resumed the song:

…an acre wide.

I heard the ma'mur and my assistant burst out laughing at the top of their voices. Then came the sound of the ma'mur upbraiding the crazy fellow: 'Watch out — your girlfriend was drowned in the canal two years ago.'

My mind was blank at this moment except for the image of the girl, framed in black, harbouring a secret to which I had so far failed to penetrate. Her secret was the clue to the entire case. But I was impelled to unearth it by an urge quite unconnected with my professional duties. There was now a personal interest as well.

The convoy went on its way till it came to a deep wide ditch brimming with water, bridged with a plank a cubit wide, cut from the trunk of a palm-tree. The ghafir was about to push my horse from behind to make it carry me across the ditch over this narrow piece of wood; but I awoke to his intention and shouted, 'You are mad, ghafir. How can I get by here on a horse?'

A look of astonishment spread over his face. 'Well, sir, you got over here last night, you and the horse and all!'

I contemplated the wooden plank with something like terror. 'Did I? So you mean to tell me that I crossed the ditch here over this plank — riding this horse? Impossible!'

'It's wide enough, and it's an intelligent horse.'

I had no further desire to listen to what the ghafir had to say. If that was what he considered a sufficiently wide passage, I had no doubt that he could cross the Sirat on the Day of Judgement riding a camel. As for the intelligence of the horse — I only had his word for it and he was not the rider. Why should I be induced to ride it on the strength of his precarious guarantee?

I quickly dismounted and crossed the ditch by the plank on foot, leaning on my stick.

31

12 October

When we got back, it was time for the session to begin. Our car approached the court, where we saw people crowded like flies at the entrance. My assistant had slumped down at my side completely prostrate and I took no further notice of him. It did not occur to me to summon him in that state of fatigue to sit through a court session with me after attending an investigation. He was not yet accustomed to a twenty-four-hour day and the instructive night which he had just spent was quite enough for him.

So I decided to deal gently with him in the early period of his service; and as soon as we came to the court, I made the driver stop and ordered him to take my assistant home.

I bade farewell to the ma'mur and alighted from the car, clearing a path between the serried ranks of men, women and children. When I entered the conference room the judge was already sitting. As soon as I saw him, my spirits dropped. There are two judges in this court and they work on alternate days. One of them lives in Cairo and travels up for the session by the first train. He always hears his cases with the utmost speed in order to catch the 11 o'clock train returning to Cairo. No matter how great the number of cases for hearing — this judge has never yet missed his train. The other judge is an excessively conscientious man who lives with his family in the district office. He is very slow in dealing with cases, for he is afraid of making mistakes through haste; and perhaps, too, he is eager to fill in time and enliven his boredom in this provincial outpost. Moreover he has no train to catch. So from early morning he sits at his desk as though he were inseparably nailed to it; and he never leaves it till just before noon. He generally resumes the session in the evening too. These sessions have always been a nightmare to me; they are a veritable sentence of imprisonment — as though I were condemned to be tied to my desk and remain immobile the whole day long. The red and green sash placed around my neck and under my armpit

32

seemed like a yoke. Was it divine vengeance for all the innocent people whom I had inadvertently sent to prison? Or is it that the consequences of our professional mistakes recoil upon us, so that we pay for them some time in our life without knowing when?

I said nothing when I saw the judge. It was clear to me that I was in for a merciless session after a night of continuous toil. I don't know what can have blurred my memory and made me imagine that it was the turn of the brisk judge to preside this morning...

I entered the court. First of all I glanced at the list and saw that we had to deal with seventy misdemeanours and forty felonies — quite sufficient to ensure an endless session with this particular judge. There were always more cases for him than for his colleagues; and the reason was quite simple. The conscientious judge never imposed a higher fine than twenty piastres for a misdemeanour, whereas his colleague raised the fine to as much as fifty piastres. People charged with misdemeanours had got to know this, and always took special care to escape from the expensive judge and patronize his more reasonably priced colleague. Today's judge had often complained and grumbled about the way his work increased in volume from one day to the next, and had never discovered the cause. I used to say to myself, 'Raise your price and you'll have a pleasant surprise.'

The usher began calling out the names of the accused from a paper which he was holding. Kuzman Effendi, the usher, was an old man with white hair and a white moustache, endowed with a presence and bearing fit for a Justice of the Supreme Court. Whenever he called anyone to the box, he was extremely majestic in his movements, gestures and voice. He would turn to the court attendant with an air of supreme authority, and that worthy fellow would echo the name outside the chamber just as he had heard it from the usher, except that he would introduce a long-drawn-out chant and an intonation like that of a street-hawker. A certain

judge had once noticed this resemblance, and said to him, 'Come, Sha'ban, are you calling out the names of defendants in crime cases or selling potatoes and black dates?'

And the man replied, 'Crime cases, potatoes, dates, it's all the same; it's all to make a living.'

The first defendant took his place. The judge, who had plunged into his papers, now raised his head, adjusted a pair of thick spectacles on his nose and said to the man before him, 'You have contravened the Slaughter of Animals Regulations by killing a sheep outside the slaughter-house.'

'Your honour, we slaughtered the sheep — saving your presence — on a very special evening (may you be granted one like it) — it was the circumcision of our little son and...'

'Twenty piastres fine! Next case!'

The usher called out a name. And so it went on — name after name — a whole succession of cases exactly similar to the first on which sentence had been pronounced. I left the judge to his verdicts and began to amuse myself by observing the people in the court... They filled all the seats and benches and overflowed on to the floor and gangways, where they sat on their haunches like cattle gazing up humbly at the judge, while he pronounced sentence like a shepherd with a staff. The judge grew weary of the succession of identical cases and shouted, 'What is all this about? Is there nothing in this court except sheep outside slaughter-houses?'

He glared at the crowd with eyes like little peas behind his spectacles, which bobbed up and down his nose. Nobody, not even himself, caught the implication of what he had said. The usher went on calling out names. The type of charge had begun to vary and we were entering a different world, for the judge was now saying to the accused, 'You are charged with having washed your clothes in the canal!'

'Your honour — may God exalt your station — are you going to fine me just because I washed my clothes?'

'It's for washing them in the canal.'

'Well, where else could I wash them?'

The judge hesitated, deep in thought, and could give no answer. He knew very well that these poor wretches had no wash basins in their village, filled with fresh flowing water from the tap. They were left to live like cattle all their lives and were yet required to submit to a modern legal system imported from abroad.

The judge turned to me and said, 'The Legal Officer! Opinion, please.'

'The state is not concerned to inquire where this man should wash his clothes. Its only interest is the application of the law.'

The judge turned his glance away from me, lowered his head, shook it and then spoke swiftly like a man rolling a weight off his shoulders: 'Fined twenty piastres. Next case.'

A woman's name was called. It was the village prostitute. She had blackened her eyelashes with the point of a match and smeared her cheeks with the glaring crimson colour which can be seen painted on boxes of Samson cigarettes. On her bare arm was tattooed the picture of a heart pierced by an arrow. She was wearing on her wrist several bracelets and armlets made of metal and coloured glass.

The judge looked at her and said, 'You are charged with having stood at the entrance of your house...'

She put her hand on her hip and shouted, 'Well, darling, is it a crime for someone to stand in front of his house?'

'You were doing it to seduce the public.'

'What a pity! By your honour's beard, I've never seen this Public — he's never called in at my place.'

'Twenty piastres. Next case.'

Kuzman Effendi summoned the next defendant. He was a middle-aged farmer of some prosperity, to judge from his blue turban, his kashmir galabieh, his cloak of 'imperial' pattern and his elastic boots of screaming yellow tint. As soon as he appeared, the judge sprang the accusation upon him: 'You, sir, are charged with not having registered your dog within the statutory period.'

The accused coughed, shook his head and mumbled as though reciting a religious formula, 'A fine age we're living in — dogs have to be "registered" like plots of land, and a great fuss is made over them!'

'Twenty piastres fine. Next case...'

The hearing of the misdemeanours continued, all in the same vein. Not a single one of the defendants showed any sign of believing in the real iniquity of whatever he had done. It was merely that fines had fallen upon them from heaven, whence all disasters proceed; they had to be paid, for so the law required. I had often tried to convince myself of the purpose of these sessions. Could one claim that these judgments had a deterrent effect when the delinquent had not the least idea of what fault he had committed?

We got through the misdemeanours and the usher called out, 'Cases of Felony.' He glanced at the list and shouted, 'Umm as-Sa'ad, daughter of Ibrahim al-Jarf.'

An old peasant woman walked slowly down the centre of the room until she reached the dais, where she stood in front of Kuzman Effendi the usher. He directed her towards the judge, at whom she gazed weakly for a while. Soon she turned away from him and stood once more with her eyes fixed on the aged usher.

The judge buried his face in the papers and asked, 'Your name?'

'Umm Sa'ad, sir.'

She appeared to address this reply to the usher, who made a sign directing her once more to face the dais. The judge questioned her: 'Your profession?'

'Woman, your honour!'

'You are charged with biting the finger of Shaikh Hasan Imara.'

She left the dais and addressed the usher again: 'I swear to you, by the honour of your white hair, that I haven't done any wrong — I swore, I gave a sacred oath that my daughter wouldn't be married for a dowry of less than twenty

gold pieces.'

The judge raised his head, adjusted his spectacles, looked at her and said sharply, 'Now then, speak to me. I'm the judge here. Did you bite him? Answer yes or no!'

'Bite him? God forbid! I've got a temper, I admit — but I don't go as far as biting people!'

'Call the witness,' the judge said to the usher.

The victim appeared — his finger bound in a sheath. The judge asked him his name and occupation, made him swear that he would tell nothing but the truth and asked him to elucidate what had happened.

'Your honour, I wasn't on one side nor on the other, and the matter arose because I generously offered to mediate.'

He relapsed into silence, as though he had completely clarified the whole matter.

The judge glared at him in repressed anger, and then upbraided him and ordered him to recount in detail what had happened. The man made a full statement to this effect:

The accused woman had a daughter called Sitt Abuha; she was wooed by a peasant named Horaisha, who offered a dowry of fifteen gold pieces. The mother refused and demanded twenty. The matter stood there until one day the suitor's brother, a young boy called Ginger, came along on his own accord and informed the bride's family, quite falsely, that the suitor had accepted their terms. He then went back to his brother and told him that the girl's family had agreed to reduce the dowry and to accept his offer. As a result of this cunning joke played on both parties, a day was appointed for reciting the Fatiha at the bride's house, and the bridegroom deputed Shaikh Hasan and Shaikh Faraj to be his witnesses.

Everybody came together and the girl's mother killed a goose. Scarcely had the meal been made ready and served to the guests when the dowry was mentioned and the trick was revealed. It was evident that the deadlock had not been solved and a quarrel flared up between the two parties. The

girl's mother began to shout and wail in the yard: 'What a dreadful calamity! How our enemies would rejoice. By the life of the Prophet, I will not let my daughter go for less than twenty gold pieces.' The woman, half-crazed, rushed in amongst the menfolk to defend her daughter's interests, fearing that the men would settle the matter in an unsatisfactory way. Shaikh Hasan was moved by the spirit of devoted zeal and did not touch the food. He began to argue with the woman, vainly trying to convince her, while his colleague, Shaikh Faraj, stretched out his hand towards the goose and began to guzzle it avidly, without entering into the impassioned dispute. It appears that the enthusiasm on each side went beyond the limits of verbal discussion, and soon Shaikh Hasan saw that his hand was not in the plate of goose but in the woman's mouth. He let forth a resounding shriek and soon the whole house was turned upside down in chaotic confusion. Shaikh Hasan grabbed his companion, pulled him violently away from the goose, and went out, gnashing his teeth with rage. His companion, who had not said a single word, had been rewarded with an excellent meal; whereas he, after all his zeal, had left the banquet hungry, with his finger bitten by the old woman...

The plaintiff went on at great length. Suddenly the judge was seized with agitation. His conscientious scruples had come to life, and he interrupted the witness, saying, as though in a soliloquy, 'I wonder if I made the witness take the oath!'

He turned to me and inquired, 'Prosecuting Counsel, did I make the witness take the oath?'

I tried hard to remember, but the judge could not banish his doubts. He shouted at the witness, 'Take the oath, sir. Say: "By Almighty God, I swear to speak the truth!"'

The man swore the oath — whereupon the judge called out, 'Begin your evidence from the beginning!'

I saw that we would never finish the session. I was utterly bored and sank, yawning, into my seat. Sleep began to play with my eyelids and there elapsed an interval the length of

38

which I cannot surmise. Suddenly I heard the judge's voice calling to me: 'Prosecution! What is the request of Prosecuting Counsel?'

I opened a pair of bloodshot eyes which requested nothing but sleep and was informed by the judge that he had just studied the medical report, which said that the injury had left a permanent infirmity — the loss of the medial parallax of the third finger. I sat up in my seat and immediately demanded a ruling of *ultra vires*. The judge turned to the old woman and said, 'The case has become a felony and within the jurisdiction of the Criminal Court.'

The old lady showed no sign of understanding this subtle distinction. In her view, a bite was a bite. How could it suddenly be transformed from a misdemeanour into a felony? (What an accursed law it is — far beyond the comprehension of these simple folk!)

The next case was called. It dealt with a violent quarrel, leading to blows, which had broken out between the father of Sitt Abuha and the family of the husband, Sayyid Horaisha — for eventually the marriage had taken place. The bridegroom had sent some of his relations with a camel to take the bride from her father's house, but her father had received them with sharp abuse, shouting in their faces, 'What? A camel? My daughter leave here on a camel? Not likely! There must be a Toumbeel.'*

The two parties began to argue about who was to pay for this newfangled device provided by modern scientific development. The argument led to the raising of sticks and the effusion of a few drops of blood — quite inevitable in a situation of this kind. Finally, a well-intentioned person produced a banknote from his pocket and hired one of the taxis which plied on the country roads.

The judge gave his ruling on the dispute, and remarked, 'Thank heavens, we've finished with the joys of matrimony. Next case.'

* Automobile.

39

The usher called out with his deep, full voice, 'Cases of detained persons!' He then recited a name. There was a clang of chains, and from a crowd of people dressed in regulation prison garb a man got up. The guard removed his fetters. From the lawyer's bench a fat effendi, with a stomach like a full water-skin, arose and said, 'I represent the defendant.'

'A case with an advocate.' I reflected in silence — he won't leave us alone before unloading all his ideas upon us — in the name of freedom of defence. I may as well close my eyes, for my head is sorely in need of rest after being awake all night.

I heard the judge addressing the prisoner: 'You are accused of having stolen a kerosene stove.'

'It is true that I found a kerosene stove at the shop entrance, but I certainly didn't steal it.'

His honour turned to the usher and called for the first witness. A man appeared, dressed in a white cap and a sleeveless tunic. He took the oath and described how he had lit a kerosene stove to make coffee for some of the customers sitting inside his shop. He was a little country grocer who sold sugar, tea and tobacco. Sometimes people would assemble in his shop as though it were a sort of café. He had put the stove, already lit, at the threshold of the door and had gone inside to bring a pot. When he emerged, he saw the accused carrying off the stove, light and all, and running away with it. The witness went on at inordinate length, invoking the confirmation of those who had been present and had joined him in chasing the thief. The judge was silent and downcast, and I knew by his demeanour that he was thinking of something else. Suddenly he looked at me and said, as though speaking to himself, 'Did I make the witness take the oath?'

I could endure no more and I snapped back in annoyance, 'Good heavens, I heard him with my own ears take the oath!'

'Are you sure?'

I thought I was going to collapse. I muttered in a low

whisper, 'Do you want me to swear that he swore the oath?'

The judge was somewhat reassured and listened to the remaining witnesses in silent attention. But the defendant could no longer contain himself, and suddenly burst out in an imploring voice, 'Your honour, is there any thief in the world who would steal a lit kerosene stove?'

The judge silenced him with a wave of the hand. 'Are you asking me? I've never worked as a thief, so how should I know?'

He turned to the defending counsel's box. The advocate rose, saying, at the top of his voice, 'Mr President, we have neither encountered nor perceived nor passed in the vicinity of a kerosene stove. The entire accusation is fabricated from beginning to end.'

He was about to proceed in this vein, but the judge interrupted him: 'Excuse me, my learned friend. The defendant himself confesses that he did find the stove at the entrance of the shop.'

The lawyer banged his fist on the desk and said, 'It is bad defence on the part of my client!'

'Does counsel imply that I should accept his excellent defence in preference to the truth pronounced by his client in open court?'

Counsel protested and raised his voice. It seemed that his only interest was to make his voice reverberate through the court, to flow with sweat and wipe it away with his handkerchief, looking at his client as if to demonstrate the trouble he was taking and the interest he was devoting in his cause. Weariness, boredom, immobile captivity at my desk — all this had made me unconscious and oblivious of what was going on around me. I buried my head in one of the files and surrendered myself to deep slumber.

13 October

The session ended at noon and I emerged from it with my nerves torn to shreds. As soon as I had taken leave of the judge, I found myself confronted with a policeman holding trays filled with 'Execution of Judgment' forms, which he gave me to sign. I automatically put my signature to the endless streams of documents. (My signature no longer bears any resemblance to my name: speed and frequency have converted it into a couple of lines flung aimlessly at the paper.) Having finished this task, I looked up, dripping with perspiration, and heard someone beating the floor with his shoe and raising his hand in salute. 'Sir, the inquiry into the shooting is waiting upstairs.'

Human endurance has its limits. I had not tasted a morsel of food or stretched myself on a bed since the day before yesterday. I could restrain myself no longer. 'Go and shoot yourself! If I were a soldier in the trenches there would be some pity for my condition and some consideration for my health!' I cried.

The man had done nothing to merit this abuse. So I left him and went off up the stairs to my office on the second floor, where I found Rim waiting at the door with her warder, and Shaikh Asfur standing nearby with his green staff. I could not imagine what he was waiting for. The spectacle of the young girl had a refreshing effect on me, like dewdrops on withered grass.

I went into my room, where I found the ma'mur, the inspector and the clerk of the court sitting with all the blithe vigour of those who have just awakened from a pleasant sleep. I saw that they had just come from their homes and were looking forward to killing time over this case, which was more entertaining than playing dominoes in the club or sucking sugar-cane outside the pharmacy. But I was unfit for anything except seven hours' uninterrupted sleep; so I informed those present that I wished to postpone the inquiry till tomorrow — to which they all agreed. Here a problem

arose of which nobody had thought: where was the girl to spend the night? She was far from her village and there was no point in her going back only to return next morning. Besides, someone interested in the case — one of the witnesses or one of the villagers — might get in touch with her and prompt her in such a way as to confuse the true issue; whereas in this police station she had no acquaintances or connections.

'It's quite a simple matter,' said the ma'mur — with an air of gratification at finding a happy and successful solution. 'The girl can sleep in my house till morning.'

We all turned on him with something like a shudder, but we soon pulled ourselves together again. Somehow the same feeling crept into the minds of everyone present at the same instant. Even Shaikh Asfur, who had slunk into the room behind me, was visibly perturbed. It was a delicate situation, for any objection on our part could only mean an aspersion on the character of his honour the ma'mur. And, on the other hand, if we delivered this gentle burden into his keeping — God alone could save the situation. Rumour told how this ma'mur had one day become infatuated with a peasant girl who came to see him with some petition. Being anxious to be alone with her, he had ordered his constable and warder to enter the prison and shave the prisoners. When they were safely inside, he locked the door behind them and kept them locked up while he was having a *tête-à-tête* with his lady. Remembering this, I could not help but reflect that, if matters took a serious turn, a heavy load would weigh on my conscience as Legal Officer for having delivered this ripe apple into those avid, slobbering jaws. The strange thing was that everybody present was silent and downcast, as though all were firmly convinced that the precious morsel was as good as devoured and digested — and there the matter ended.

The ma'mur, anxious to reassure us, said, 'What I mean is that she ought to be in a safe place — with my wife and children.'

43

I could see no course open to me except to submit. I left the place and went home, where I had a quick meal. I then went to bed and dropped into a deep slumber, from which I awoke at midnight. I arose, feeling thirsty, and quaffed a draught of water from the earthenware pot on the windowsill. I bethought myself of the girl, imagining her in our friend's house, and all thought of sleep vanished from my head. I wished that a case would now crop up, obliging me to attend to it, together with the ma'mur. But cases are like cats — when you call them they refuse to come, and when you shoo them away they rub themselves against your feet. I could think of nothing to do. I was now besieged by fears and apprehensions and the night drew on, long and tedious, while I sat yearning for daybreak. I tried to occupy my mind by writing my diary but the pen was inert in my hand. My eyes rested on piles of cases — misdemeanours, felonies and petitions — all the influx of the two preceding days. The Registrar had sent them to me to read and register and present to the court, with the charges properly drafted. But I felt no inclination to work. I went across, opened the window and breathed in the moist night air. I looked at the stars shining over the vast silence of the sleeping countryside, like watchful eyes scrutinizing the hidden mysteries of life.

Suddenly I conceived the idea of putting on my clothes, going down into the street and walking round the ma'mur's house. What a mad notion! How could I do any such thing? What if the sentry caught me? He would probably recognize me and apologize — but he would tell people all about it, and the news would spread and there would be a dreadful scandal. So there was nothing for it but to wait for the morning — and whatever it would bring in its train.

Finally, however, fortune smiled on me and sent a telephone message. I read it hurriedly and it was plainly a trivial incident of the sort which does not usually involve our getting up at night: 'While goods train No. 209 was passing Kilo 17 on the narrow Delta line, during a shunting

44

operation, an iron nail was found on the track. Attempted damage by person, or persons, unknown, etc, etc.'

The ma'mur had appended a note at the bottom of the message, deputing the inspector to go to the scene of the incident and to inform the Legal Officer. This meant that he himself had no intention of getting up and did not wish me to get up either. But how could I let this heaven-sent opportunity slip? I had no dearer wish tonight than to disturb my rest — and that of his honour the ma'mur. I dressed instantly, ordered the car and drove to the ma'mur's house. I sent someone to bang loudly on the door and inform him of my arrival. Soon he put his head out of the window: 'A little nail — and you want us all to go there at night?'

I leant out of the window of the car. 'Yes — even if it's only a needle. As long as it's a deliberate act by somebody, it counts as a felony. Observe that it's an attempted derailment — the most dangerous crime in the world! Your presence is essential.'

'Why — I've deputed the inspector to act for me!'

'It is essential that you be present in person.'

'Tonight, it's impossible, really. Not tonight. Actually I'm dead tired!'

'We're all just as tired, but duty is duty, you know.'

He thought for a moment in silent fury. Seeing my stubborn determination, he was afraid to oppose me officially; so he acquiesced and asked me to wait a while till he dressed. He came down and sat beside me in the car, puffing with anger. I noticed that Shaikh Asfur had not turned up: despite the sound of the horn, no trace of him had appeared. On this occasion, the ma'mur was deep in thought and did not notice the Shaikh's absence. After a prolonged silence, he said, 'Yes, of course — duty is duty. But — dash it all — a nail...!'

I closed my eyes to avoid answering him.

'God bless the Legal Officer who was here before you. In a murder case he only required two witnesses, and nothing

45

more. He would then close his report, turn to me and say, "Well, the murdered man wasn't my father or brother. Come along, old man, let's go and have a drink…"'

I made no comment and uttered no sound during the whole journey until we reached Kilo 17, where we found the railway workers, the goods train and its driver. The deputy umdah handed me the nail and pointed to a wagon laden with bags of cotton, freshly cut. I took the nail between my fingers and began to examine it.

The ma'mur, who was standing behind me, said, with a grin, 'Where was the stoker when the engine broke?'

I knew that he was alluding facetiously to a song beginning with that sentence which had been all the rage thirty years ago when Shafika the Copt had been the star of the Egyptian stage. The engine-driver, however, heard the remark, and took it literally. He stepped forward and said, 'Nothing was broken, sir. At the time of the accident I was at the brakes. I applied the brakes immediately.'

He went on expressing his views at length and in detail. According to his notion, the inhabitants of this area were simple-minded folk, probably descended from the villagers who, when a train first appeared, invited it to lunch and gave it food and drink. It was not improbable that one of these villagers had now been moved by a sense of fun and curiosity to put this nail on the railway track to see what the train would do and how it would deal with the situation — whether it would fall on its side or on its face.

One of the mechanics, however, came forward with another solution: it was not a case of simple-mindedness or stupidity at all. It was an act of vengeance against the Company. The inhabitants of these areas got their livelihood by extracting stones from the hills and loading them on donkeys and camels for sale to contractors. The Anglo-Delta Railway Company had then come on the scene and laid a line quite recently all the way to the hilltop, thus securing a monopoly of this form of revenue and snatching the very

stones from the hungry mouths of these famished paupers.

Whichever cause was the true one, the fact remained that the culprit was unknown — and unlikely to be discovered. We closed the case by putting the nail in an envelope, sealing it with red wax and enclosing it with the relevant papers, going through the entire rigmarole of formality, which was the essence of our 'trade'. The morning dew had begun to fall and the ma'mur decided to draw up his report in the umdah's 'apartment'. I asked how far that was and the deputy umdah replied, 'Just a stone's throw, sir.'

We took his word for it and set off on foot, walking until our joints nearly cracked. We arrived just as the dawn prayer was being announced in the tiny local mosque. I left the ma'mur to fling curses at the deputy umdah for his remark about 'a stone's throw', and busied myself with opening the summary of evidence and interrogating the witnesses until I had finished with them all and was ready to close my Report. Whereupon I noticed the movement of a table being laid and food being prepared; and there was his honour the ma'mur bobbing up and down, looking at the table and coming in and out without my having the least idea of what was keeping him so busy. Eventually I heard him talking to the umdah in a corner of the room: 'Now, listen, his excellency the Legal Officer doesn't like mutton or chicken for breakfast, or anything like that. But there's no objection to a few pigeons in rice, with dried biscuit and whipped pastry. If there are a few light roasted chickens with it, there's no harm. Of course, some curdled milk is always good for the health. There's no harm in some eggs fried in cream. That's quite enough. See that you don't make anything more. The Legal Officer has a small appetite. If you have some waxed honey, bring it in. There's nothing against a couple of cream cheeses and a plate of cakes and dainties. The whole point is: something good and light. You know better than anyone what is required...'

I was dumbfounded by this discourse and blushed helplessly.

I decided that the best thing to do would be to go as quickly as possible. I wrapped up my papers hurriedly. But the ma'mur had observed me and was wise to my intention. He came over to me rapidly. 'Inquiry all over?' he asked.

'Some time ago.'

He looked at the table, on which nothing had yet been laid, and turned to me again: 'Have all the witnesses given their evidence?'

'Every one of them.'

'Not a single one left?'

'Not a quarter of one.'

He turned and ran out briskly. In a few minutes he came back, dragging one of the villagers by his scarf. He pushed the man in front of me and pointed to him: 'A very important witness. He's got some evidence to give.'

I showed some scepticism about the value of the man's evidence and indicated my desire to be content with the witnesses whom I had already interrogated. But the ma'mur urged me insistently to listen to this witness as well — for he had evidence of the greatest importance to give. I spread my papers out again and began to put my first question, whereupon the umdah appeared, followed by his servants, who put food on the table. Our host's voice was then heard inviting us to breakfast. I excused myself on the grounds of weak health and my habit of abstaining from food in the morning. The umdah swore a mighty oath in an effort to persuade me and advanced with the ma'mur to carry me bodily from my place. I soon found myself seated at table. I had to give in, so I began to observe these gentlemen — including the ma'mur — chewing, guzzling and swallowing, entirely absorbed in themselves and oblivious of my lack of appetite. I got up and slipped away from them after a short interval. I went back to my place, waiting idly for a time, and turned over the pages of my Report, until they had filled their bellies and demolished all the food on the table, and had got up, wiping their hands on the tablecloth, which had

not seen any soap for about two years. The ma'mur approached me, belching loudly: 'I think we may as well go back, as the inquiry is over.'

I pointed to the witness whom he had brought to me — and evidently forgotten. 'When we have interrogated your important witness.'

He answered immediately, 'He is not of any importance at all.'

He turned from me towards the peasant: 'Have you any information for us, my man?'

'Nay,' he answered, in a country drawl.

'God confound the silly ass; he hasn't any information at all. Come on, sir, let's go back to our village.'

We got up to go, for the sun had already risen. As soon as we reached the police-post, the sergeant came up with a message from the Government Hospital, saying that the injured man, Kamar al-Dawla Alwan, had recovered consciousness and could be interrogated now. We hurried off to the hospital, regardless of all else, fearing lest he might suffer a relapse into unconsciousness, in which case we would never extract the secret of the crime.

We entered the hospital and asked for the chief surgeon. We were informed that he was in the operating theatre. We went along the corridor leading to the theatre. On our way we encountered little beds and trolleys being wheeled along the asphalt floor like porters' barrows at railway stations. We saw sterilizing stoves on rollers being pushed along amidst rising billows of steam. Busy hospital orderlies in white suits pushed the trollies with their load of bodies on their way to eternity, into the dreadful chamber and out again, showing on their faces no sign of interest in life or death. I stopped for a moment in distraction, feeling as though I were in a station surrounded by trains. Yes, it was exactly like that. Was I not in the station from which the sick set out for the other world? I happened to turn my gaze towards the hospital gate, where I saw the sentry on guard

shooing away swarms of women in their black clothes and their blue amulets, thronging around and shouting in voices broken by anxious sobs. Then I knew that he would soon fling a corpse to them; for every day a corpse or two would be thrown outside these walls, an offering to the grief that crouched, waiting by the gate.

The door of the operating theatre opened and an orderly came out with a pail containing congealed blood and pieces of flesh, like the entrails of a sheep. I looked at it and was informed that all this had just come out of the belly of a woman now lying on the operating table under chloroform. I stood transfixed and paralysed. The ma'mur went up and demanded, in my name, an immediate interview with the chief surgeon. The orderly went off and soon returned, opening the door of the operating theatre to admit us. I pulled myself together and went in, followed by my colleague. The chief surgeon received me with a smile. Dressed in his white jacket, he was still leaning over the operating table with his sleeves rolled up, holding something like a pair of tongs. He was surrounded by a group of his non-medical friends in their ordinary attire. I recognized some of the city notables amongst them. I approached and looked at what lay before me. It was a girl's body, on whose abdomen he had just made a long incision, reaching from the chest to the lowest part of her stomach. The 'tongs' in his hand were gathering up the severed skin and sewing it up with what looked like little nails. The surgeon did this with astonishing speed, chatting the while, joking and laughing with his guests like a conjuror glorying in his sleight of hand and professional dexterity. I glanced at the girl's ashen face: she looked as though she were dead. I saw that the skin of her abdomen was studded with a long row of nails like the leather of a shoe in the hands of the cobbler. I had a feeling of great dizziness in my head and feared that I would faint. I leant on the side of the operating table and the surgeon, observing my pallor, left the patient and glanced

50

at me anxiously. I hurried from the theatre, saying, in a half-choked voice, 'I'll be waiting for you after the operation, doctor.'

The ma'mur asked what was wrong with me and I could not explain. I had seen many post-mortem operations, and had often watched bodies being cut up and bellies being split open without being affected by the sight. But those were lifeless bodies. I suppose that I was moved so violently because I was now seeing living bodies being treated like inanimate matter. Or perhaps some vestige of the smell of chloroform, diffused in the air of the operating theatre, had reached my nostrils when I approached the girl's body.

The fresh air outside the operating theatre restored my energy. We sat waiting in the surgeon's office drinking coffee, which had been ordered by the chief hospital attendant, until the chief surgeon appeared and conducted us courteously to the ward in which the wounded man lay.

We passed with him along corridors crowded with beds, since the wards could not contain all their unhappy inmates. We saw the convalescents in their wide blue tunics avidly devouring their porridge from aluminium pots, staring at us as we passed with the chief surgeon, like monkeys in the zoo gazing at their keepers and visitors.

We came to Kamar al-Dawla's bed and found him prostrate and motionless. The chief surgeon pulled a piece of paper from the top of the bed on which were recorded the phases of his illness. He read us some medical symptoms, to which I paid scant attention. 'The point is,' I said, 'can we interrogate him?'

'I think so — if you make it very brief,' replied the surgeon in a low voice. He went to the patient and called him gently. The man opened a pair of lustreless eyes, which seemed to perceive nothing and to have no power of focusing on anything. I drew near and spoke: 'Kamar al-Dawla — who shot you?'

He did not reply. I repeated the question and he opened

his lips, but emitted no sound. I pressed him for an answer, and he made a visible effort to pronounce one single word: 'Rim!'

I was taken aback for a while. I turned leftwards and rightwards and found the ma'mur and the clerk of the court looking just as interested and astonished as myself. I again looked into the patient's eyes and said, 'Make your point clear, Kamar.'

No reply.

'Do you mean to say that Rim herself...?'

He did not stir.

'Kamar! Alwan! Speak to me: you've got to speak. Just one word: Who shot you? Who was it?'

But we were demanding the impossible. He had shut his eyes and his forehead was damp with sweat. The chief surgeon pulled me by the hand and said, 'That's enough.'

I looked at the ma'mur in desperation. 'Is that all?'

Had we achieved anything useful? We had been in a clearer position when we came in than we were now. We only had a single word which his dry mouth had uttered with great effort. I wished that he hadn't uttered it at all.

14 October

I left the ma'mur to go about his business and went back to my office in the Legal Department. My assistant had heard of my return and came in as though he were longing to set eyes on me. But he was angry with me for overlooking him during the investigation of our night case. I realized that I had indeed forgotten him entirely. My eagerness to take the ma'mur along that night had undoubtedly made me oblivious of all else. Anyway, it was a trivial case which had served nothing except the ma'mur's belly and had harmed nothing except the umdah's pocket. Poor umdahs — I've often pitied them...

The court attendant, Shaikh Khamis, appeared and I asked him for a glass of weak tea. I turned towards my assistant, who advanced upon me talking away, apparently for the sake of talking, as though he were starved of speech. Solitude had nearly killed him during my absence. He was fed up with the village. He couldn't find a single café here worthy to be patronized by a man of his position. The nearest approach was the shop of the Greek grocer called Tanacci, in front of which were two wooden tables and two wicker chairs. The villagers called it 'The Buffet'. Even this Greek wore a peasant's galabieh and had no trace of European origin except the colour of his eyes and hair. Where was a young man to amuse himself? Where was he to spend his time? This young man had recently come up from Cairo, where there were lights, noise and cabarets. And now there was hardly anything for him to see except a few buildings — most of which were tumbledown — and some little hovels thatched with cotton stalks and maize twigs, in which the fellahin lived. Their dusty brown colour was suggestive of mud, manure and the dung of cattle; they stood crowded and huddled together in villages and farms, scattered among the plantation as though they too were heads of cattle let loose in the fields. And these bits of houses, in whose interior the fellahin lived like worms, were all that there was to see in these parts.

To make him still more wretched, there was this stillness which descended on the village after sunset; thereafter there was no sound except the lowing of oxen, the barking of dogs, the braying of donkeys and the creaking of water-wheels, pumps and hydraulic machines, apart from the sound of shots let off in the dead of night by private or official watchmen trying to frighten other people, or to keep up their own courage. My poor assistant needed something to cure him of his boredom. But there is no cure for village life except marriage or riotous living, or reading, or writing a diary, as I do whenever I can. My young friend had thought

of frequenting the club — but he knew nothing about the local club. The 'club' was an honorific bestowed on an old room reached by a wooden ladder and lit by a petrol lamp, which was the only article worthy of respect in the whole room. The members of the club, of course, were the officials, the local doctor, some of the notables and government employees and the owner of the pharmacy. Their only occupation in that place was to play cards or dominoes and to gossip about other people. I was doubtful whether it was proper for a representative of the law to join this merry band. I had told my assistant that I personally preferred a member of the legal staff to keep far away from all that if he wished to earn general respect.

I shall never forget the day when the officials of this area and the local judge invited me to a dinner party in honour of a colleague who was being posted elsewhere. Unable to refuse, I went along. There were bottles of whisky amongst plates of food on the table, and someone had filled my glass and that of the judge. That dignitary was a trifle careless and drank too much. He began to chatter and giggle rather inappropriately. The ma'mur, who was also drunk, leant over towards me and whispered in my ear, 'His honour has lost his dignity!' I didn't wish to hear any more of that, so I slipped away and went home quickly, without being noticed by the other guests, busy with their cups. From that day onwards I had not set foot in the club. My assistant was won over to my way of thinking but I wished to expatiate on the matter so as to make him still more careful. At that moment, however, Haj Khamis came in with a glass. As soon as I saw it, I exclaimed, 'What are you giving me to drink? Better let me have some copying-ink and have done with it.'

'By the life of the Prophet, your excellency, I've been an attendant at the court for twenty years: believe me, I've known all sorts of people and officials. Take my word for it — there's nothing like tea with a bitter Fernet taste for

these courts!'

I hesitated a moment, then lost control and burst out, 'Court tea and court work — it's all bitter, and that's all there is to it. Pass me a cup.'

He put it before me and went off. As soon as I had taken the first sip, the door opened to admit Abd al-Maqsud Effendi, the Head of the Criminal Section. I never could stand the sight of him.

'Four cases of "suspicious circumstances".'

'Bring them in.'

He went away and sent me the policeman who was in charge of summaries of evidence and the custody of prisoners. We began reading the papers before summoning the accused. I took three cases myself. A quick glance at one file told me that it was insignificant, so I handed it to my assistant and said, 'Theft of a jar of maize. We'll never find you an easier case than this. Interrogate this fellow — you'll find that he'll plead guilty for sure.'

My assistant showed some signs of agitation. It was the first time he was going to interrogate a suspect. He took the file from me and began to read it word by word, and then read the whole thing again; it was not more than five pages. I had finished my share of the files, which was twice as big as his, and looked up to find him still absorbed in preparing exhaustive summaries, and comments on the summaries, and questions carefully prepared beforehand as missiles to be hurled at the purloiner of the jar of maize. I smothered a laugh. I had behaved in exactly the same way at the beginning of my judicial career. Fate had been harsher to me than to this young man and had afflicted me with a complicated forgery case to mark the début of my career in investigation. I shall never forget how agitated I was when the accused forger appeared before me with all his resourcefulness, smoothness of tongue and long experience of judges. The carefully prepared questions went clean out of my mind and I could find nothing to say. The man stood before me,

expectant and calm, waiting for me to open my mouth or for the Almighty to prompt me with a question. Sweat poured from me as I realized that the accused was more happy, more self-contained and confident than I was myself. I had the feeling that he was inwardly laughing at me. The clerk of the court was an old man, with long training, who had certainly met dozens of new assistants like me in the course of his life. He sized me up and quickly came to my rescue by prompting me with the proper opening questions. I accepted his aid with haughty arrogance, refusing to show openly that I had any need of his intervention. There are many worthy old clerks like him — unhonoured and unsung. I once heard one of them, pointing to an eminent judge, saying, 'We teach them the job and they get on in the world and rise to be judges and counsellors, while the likes of us stay put, not moving an inch up or down, like donkeys with a load of hay.'

All this came back to me as I looked at my assistant's face. I thought that I had better supervise his infant steps myself: so I told him to put his summaries away and to press the bell. He did so, whereupon the court usher appeared at the door and I ordered him to bring in the first defendant. In came an old peasant, his chest sprouting with bluish-white tufts of hair like the coat of an aged hyena. I told my assistant to put whatever questions occurred to him and not to be afraid, as I could come to his aid if he was held up. The young man blushed and stammered; then he made a great effort, glared at the accused, and said, 'Did you steal the jar of maize?'

The answer came promptly from the depth of his stomach: 'I was hungry.'

The assistant looked at me and spoke with a note of triumph in his voice: 'The accused admits the theft.'

'Who says that I deny it?' said the man, with complete candour. 'It is quite true — I was hungry, so I went down to one of the fields and took a jar full.'

The pen in my assistant's hand stopped writing. He could think of nothing to ask after that. He turned to me, imploringly. I looked at the prisoner and asked, 'Why don't you work, my man?'

'Your honour, give me work and then tell me off if I don't jump at it. Poor chaps like us, one day we find something and the next ten days we find only starvation.'

'In the eyes of the law you are charged with theft.'

'Your honour, we have every respect for the law. But the law can see what goes on and must know that I'm flesh and blood and must have something to eat.'

'Have you anyone to stand bail for you?'

'I am all alone in the world.'

'Can you pay a guarantee?'

'If I had the money, I'd use it to get some food.'

'If you pay fifty piastres bail, you can be released at once.'

'Fifty piastres? Heavens alive, sir, I haven't seen what money looks like for two months! I've forgotten what half a piastre looks like. I don't even know if it still has a hole in the middle or if they've made it solid.'

I turned towards my assistant and dictated the text of my judgment: 'The accused to be confined in preventive custody for four days, with the option of renewal. Make him a file and an identity slip.'

The man kissed the palm and back of his hand gratefully. 'So what? Prison is just fine. At least we are assured a bite of food. Good morning!'

He crept out, his wrists handcuffed. My assistant calmed down and evinced relief as his prisoner departed. I called the next case. The same policeman appeared with a colleague, and together they opened the doors of my office wide and dragged in more than thirty men, women and children, tied together with a rope; for they couldn't find iron handcuffs in the station for so many people. When I saw them, I could not restrain a shout of surprise. 'Good Lord, is this herd of cattle going off to the Saturday market? Untie them, constable!'

The guards loosened the bonds, saying, 'Your honour, we searched their houses and found contraband there. There are some more people of the district being held for examination by authority of the police and the Investigation Department.'

I glanced at the band of poor wretches and recalled mentally what I had read about their case in the papers before me. 'Contraband?'

The policeman came forward to explain. 'Clothing, your honour.'

I remembered everything. What I had just read described how a big van had passed laden with heavy bags full of various cotton and woollen garments, including jackets, waistcoats and trousers, and all sorts of leather footwear destined for one of the well-known department stores in Cairo. The van with all this merchandise had passed by night over the canal bridge facing the village, and a bag full of clothing had fallen into the water. It remained at the bottom of the canal until the water-level became low and the goods were revealed above the surface. The whole ill-clad village rushed to the treasure, the like of which they had never beheld. Scores of hands fought to get near the bag lying in the mud and began to drag out whatever came to hand. If it happened to be a pair of trousers, it was put on at once over a blue galabieh. If it was a cloth jacket, the finder got into it, despite the tunic he was already wearing. If it was a pair of shiny shoes, it was put on the finder's feet without socks. The whole village rushed along the streets in extreme jubilation, shouting, 'There are clothes in the water — clothes in the water!' Finally, the police saw them, begrudged them their good fortune and suspected that it must be 'stolen goods'. The matter intrigued them and they finally discovered what had occurred.

I decided first of all to question them in a body, hoping to obtain a confession, which would make my task easier. I embraced them all in a single glance and said, 'Did you steal

58

the clothes?'

A deep, restrained voice emerged from the crowd: 'Not at all. By God, we haven't stolen anything, and don't know the meaning of the word. The water washed the bag up to us and each one of us took his share.'

'His share?' I retorted quickly. 'Do you think that the bag was owned by the water and had no legal owner?'

The man replied in a deep calm voice, 'It never occurred to us that there were any owners, your honour. God bless you, sir — have pity on these poor fellahin.'

'It's a question of law; and the law is explicit. Anyone who finds the property of another, and keeps it with intent to take possession thereof, shall be regarded as a thief. Do you understand?'

'We understand, sir... but... well, there were the clothes before our eyes washed up by the water, and we are all naked, saving your presence...'

'Do you think there is anarchy in the world, my man? Don't you realize that there's such a thing as law and government?'

The man's patience was evidently strained. 'Haven't we suffered enough from the government? It doesn't clothe us and doesn't leave us free to clothe ourselves.'

'I have no choice but to lock you up!'

'But your honour, you searched our houses and took the clothes from us. Joyful families are now in tears and we are back where we started. We owe nothing and nothing is owed to us. Is there still any need to lock anybody up?'

'I can release you on payment of bail.'

'Payment? Why the fellahin are absolutely destitute, your honour!'

'Oh, for heaven's sake, I've got a headache and it's a waste of time to argue with people like you. The law is quite explicit and I am bound by legal texts tighter than the ropes on your hands. The question for me is above all a question of law. All the accused are to be imprisoned provisionally

for four days, subject to renewal. Records to be made accordingly. Take them away!'

They all trooped out in a long column. A man at the end of the line could be heard muttering, 'They lock us up because the Lord clothed us…!'

All was now peaceful; but a dreadful stench had spread through the room. I summoned the attendant and ordered him to open the windows. He did so, muttering a curse about white buffaloes which ought not to be brought into courtrooms. I turned to my assistant and found him downcast and thoughtful. I was possessed by curiosity to know what he was feeling at that moment. Was he at all affected? Was there any remnant left of the sensitiveness and fine feeling with which we all begin our official work in the provinces — or was it all dying out? At that moment, however, there was a violent thud of a stick against the door. I recognized the ma'mur's knock and, sure enough, our friend came in panting and exclaiming, 'The girl, Rim!'

'What about her?' Despite myself, I spoke with great eagerness.

The ma'mur made himself comfortable in a chair while I impatiently waited for him to utter. He turned towards the attendant at the door: 'Bring me something to drink, for God's sake!'

He took out his artificial silk handkerchief and wiped his face and head, while I was on hot coals with excitement. Finally, he turned to me and spoke: 'She has disappeared!'

I glared at him closely. 'Are you serious?'

'She's run off with that dog of a Shaikh.'

'Shaikh Asfur?'

'Yes, confound him!'

'And what have you done about it?'

'I ordered the Investigation Section to follow the track at once on all the country lanes.'

We sat in silence, each one wrapped in his own thoughts.

60

15 October

The ma'mur did not stay long; he soon went off and I lost all touch with him. I kept trying to reach him by telephone at the police post, but nobody knew where he was. All that we knew about him was that he had not returned. I waited for him all day to find out what had happened. But night drew on, the sun set and my patience became exhausted. I went over to the police post myself, but could get no satisfaction. Somebody suggested that he might have gone to the club, as this was his usual time for sitting there. Without hesitation I made for the club, where the members received me at first with some astonishment and then hurriedly offered me the only sound chair in the room as a token of respect. I asked about the ma'mur and was told that they had not seen him and were surprised that he had not appeared at the club before. When they heard from me that he had gone out with the inspector that morning in the Ford and had not come back, they all shouted with one voice, 'We're lost and our money's lost — God alone can save us!'

At first I could not grasp what they meant; but when I chanced to look at the table and saw the cards spread out on it in preparation for a game, I understood at once. I remembered being told that the ma'mur had never known what it was to lose a game in this club. At the beginning of the month he was accustomed to win the salaries of all the officials. For the rest of the month he would go on lending them whatever they needed for their food and subsistence, so that they would not perish from hunger before payday. He would then play them again, take their new salaries and lend them enough to live on for the whole month. And so it went on. They had grown accustomed and reconciled to this life and would console themselves by saying, 'Whether the money is in our pockets or the ma'mur's pocket, the result is the same.'

They were terrified of one thing only: that was when the ma'mur went off to play against another post with the money

of the village. For he sometimes grew bored with playing these bankrupt wretches who had nothing left, and would select a few of the best players and go off with them to the neighbouring village — just like a touring football team. Sometimes the ma'mur would go off alone or with the inspector to the nearest village, play a couple of rubbers and come back. At other times they would receive a team from other villages in their club. At these heated contests between one village and another the ma'mur's pocket, and thereby the salaries of the entire district, would be exposed to danger.

However, I soon restored their peace of mind by saying that the ma'mur had probably gone off on work connected with a case which was occupying our attention. They calmed down and sat for a moment in courteous and respectful silence. They then began to talk and gossip as we drank coffee; eventually one of them spoke in welcoming terms: 'It is very auspicious to have the visit of his honour the Legal Officer; his honour the judge has kept away from the club for some time. All because of a misunderstanding.'

I looked at the speaker and something in my interrogative gaze encouraged him to continue: 'Ah yes. A misunderstanding between him and the ma'mur.' He went on chatting briskly: 'It all started with a dispute between their wives. The judge's wife fell out with the ma'mur's wife.'

I looked down in silent contemplation. The assembled company thought that I was anxious to listen further. One of them proceeded to talk away: 'The latest version is that they went up to the roofs of their houses and abused each other in the choicest terms. The ma'mur's wife, wishing to enrage her rival, went and put on the jacket of her husband's uniform, with its crown and star — and actually covered her head with his cap — and said at the top of her voice, "You don't have any escort worth mentioning — just an old usher in a cloth robe, a broken-down fellow with dyed hair. But the ma'mur has a post full of guards and soldiers under our command giving us a salute." Whereupon the judge's

wife went down, put on the official red sash over her dress and emerged, saying, "May your tongue be cut off, you silly fool! You certainly have command of a couple of miserable guards. But who else is there in the whole town who can lock people up and hang them and say, 'The court has decided'...?'"

I found it rather embarrassing to listen to this chatter. As soon as I had finished my coffee, I put down the cup quietly, got up, said farewell and went away.

I walked home, deep in thought, moving slowly, for I felt little desire to confine myself between four walls with trays full of late petitions, and bury my nose in dusty files. I was still preoccupied with the ma'mur's absence. Had he found her? If so, where had he gone? And what had happened to Shaikh Asfur?

The most extraordinary feature of the situation was that this Asfur creature could have come along and plucked such a lovely flower without our noticing him. The fact was that we had paid no attention to him. He had managed with brilliant dexterity to snatch her away from the ma'mur. From the ma'mur, mark you; not merely from me! Even more remarkable was the fact that the girl should have obeyed him and gone off with him of her own free will. For it was certain that he had not compelled her to go or carried her off against her will by force. What was the secret of this strange and potent influence, seeing that he hardly knew her and there had been no long association between them? Was it he who had induced her to escape? But why should she do so? Was she guilty of something? Could this astonishing beauty be guilty of crime? Or were we the guilty ones in thinking evil of her, despite her beauty? It is always difficult for me to think of beauty dissociated from virtue; true beauty and true virtue are identical. And yet Kamar al-Dawla, when asked who had assaulted him, muttered a single word, whose deadly echo still resounded in my ears: 'Rim!' In that case why had the girl screamed and recoiled when she first heard

of the crime? Was it mere acting and dissimulation? That night her moaning had rent my heart; and I could not doubt that the ma'mur, who was, at the very least, experienced in the ways of the village women, had been affected in exactly the same way. If the guile of a little slip of a girl like that could succeed against people like us, we ought to be tied up in a cattle ranch instead of being confronted with human souls whose inner secrets we were supposed to unravel.

As these reflections beguiled me, my feet led me by chance to the hospital. I passed the big gate and my careless glance fell on the usual scene — men, women and boys of the village squatting there. I paid no heed to them. But I had scarcely left the cluster of people before I stopped in sheer astonishment. At the foot of the wall, a little apart from the crowd, I observed Shaikh Asfur sitting on the ground, in silence, scratching the soil with the end of his stick; and near him — the girl, resting her head on the wall, either out of sheer fatigue or in deep grief. I understood everything now. She had come to the hospital to ask about the condition of the patient and had taken the crazy old man as a helper, companion and guide. Our intelligence should have led us to this obvious point. But what was I to do now? I was alone. My sole authority rested in the police, to whom I could issue orders. The only course was to return to the station and send some men to bring them both back.

I walked quickly so that they should not discover that I had seen them and run away from me in fright. As I drew away from the place, I reflected that Shaikh Asfur must undoubtedly know all the secrets of the case; or at least he must have discovered the girl's secret; his piercing eyes must have plunged into the very depths of her dark soul. But would he tell us anything? He himself was a locked mystery. I could never make up my mind if he was really a simpleton or if something lay behind his innocent exterior.

I reached the office and saw the Ford drawn up at the gate; so I knew that the ma'mur must have returned. I burst

hurriedly into his rooms and found him prostrate on the sofa, his tarbush off, and the earthenware water jug held to his mouth as he drank from it in great gulps, while sweat poured down his forehead. As soon as he saw me, he shouted, 'It's absolute witchcraft, I tell you! The dog of a Shaikh must have bewitched the girl. Just imagine! From early morning, right up to now, there isn't a single field in the district — not a single sugar plantation or water-wheel or mill or hamlet or yard or canal or ground or path or country road or flaming hell — which we haven't turned upside down and searched inch by inch. If they had been turned into birds of the field or fish in the sea, we would have found them. But the curse of it is...'

'The curse of it is that they're a few yards from here, my dear fellow.'

The ma'mur put the jar on the ground and stared at me, gaping. 'What?'

I replied rather sharply, 'Birds and fishes — eh! The man and the girl are at the hospital gate at this moment!'

'The hospital?'

'Oh, come on, my dear fellow, tell a policeman to go and get them from there. No more nonsense...'

Before I could finish my sentence the ma'mur leaped to his feet, exultantly, and shouted in a resounding voice that re-echoed through the office, 'Sergeant Abd al-Nebi!'

A giant of a man emerged from the region of the stables, clad in a white tunic and slacks. He raised his hand in salute. 'Sir?'

'Go with two men to the hospital immediately and take handcuffs with you...'

After due hesitation, the sergeant interrupted him, saying, 'The stable is open, your honour, and the men are bringing the fodder and straw for the horses...'

'You horse, carry out your orders!' screamed the ma'mur. 'I don't care a hoot if the horses don't sleep. I told you to go immediately!'

65

I left the ma'mur to give his instructions to his subordinate and went off to my office, expecting him to follow me with the wanted people when he had arrested them. I never enjoy investigations in the police station, where I am not 'at home'; for the ma'mur is the man in authority there, and I don't enjoy being under his wing during my work: especially in such a case as this and in the presence of that child. So I left hurriedly and sent somebody to fetch the clerk. I was soon in my room, seated at my desk, looking impatiently at the door and waiting for the girl's arrival with as much eagerness as for a romantic rendez-vous.

I heard a knock at my door. The ma'mur entered and immediately asked me about the two wanted witnesses; I replied that I had seen no one. He sat down, informing me that he had sent for them; and he, too, began staring at the door and twisting his moustache. My clerk brought my papers and spread them out before me. We all got busy with our preparations. Suddenly we heard a dragging sound from the corridor and the noise of heavy feet and an iron clang. The door was knocked upon and flung open and Shaikh Asfur was thrown into our midst, alone. His hands were fettered, and the corporal was behind him, carrying the Shaikh's long stick. I experienced a deep anxiety and felt that the ma'mur shared my mood. It was he who got in first with his question to the corporal: 'And the girl?'

'We found this man alone, so we arrested him, sir.'

'Alone!'

The ma'mur and I spoke simultaneously, with mingled regret, astonishment and anger. The ma'mur was beyond himself with rage and bellowed at Shaikh Asfur, 'The girl!'

The man made no movement and replied with calm restraint, 'Whose girl?'

The ma'mur gave him a terrifying glance. 'Damn you, sir, you've been smoking hashish! I know this hashish racket — you can't fool me!'

He was about to give Asfur a violent punch, but I stopped

66

him in time. I ordered the Shaikh to approach me and, when he obeyed, I asked him gently, 'Wasn't Rim with you?'

'Not at all,' he answered, without a trace of hesitation. I understood that his gimlet eyes had caught sight of me when I passed the hospital gate. He had been sharp enough to anticipate events and had lost no time in hiding the girl. Alternatively, it may have been that my own sight had deceived me and that Rim had not been beside him at all, but that my own imagination had been so swamped by the atmosphere of the girl that it had projected her image and clothing on to one of the other women waiting at the gate. Everything was possible. But where had Rim gone in that case? Why should I be more suspicious of the evidence of my eyes than of this cunning old rogue? I shouted at him abruptly, 'Come here, you!'

'At your service!'

'Who are you?'

He stared at me uncomprehendingly. I repeated my words with violent emphasis.

He replied, 'I... I'm Asfur. I pick grain above the earth, and serve my Lord beneath it...'

'Talk sense, man — your name?'

'Asfur.' He pointed to his handcuffs and shouted, 'Release me. By the love of the Prophet, somebody let me loose!'

I ordered the constable to undo his hands and went on to interrogate him sharply: 'Your profession?'

The old man hesitated for a moment in silence; he then sighed from the bottom of his heart and threw his head back. His eyes became transfixed as though they were staring at some object having no existence in the tangible world; and then he lifted up his voice and sang:

> Once I was a fisherman,
> A game all sportsmen like;
> I plunged into the water
> To catch a little pike;

67

> The fish were wonderful and odd,
> Swimming everywhere;
> The first one was a slippery cod,
> The next a turbot fair.

'All right,' interrupted the ma'mur, '*All right!* What about the one that was drowned in the storm a couple of years back — was that a cod or a turbot?'

The old man ignored him and made no reply. He went on with his song:

> The first one was a slippery cod,
> The next a turbot fair,
> The third, a creature graced by God,
> Became the sailor's snare.

He sighed deeply over the concluding sentence, and his voice took on a strange significance which made me shiver slightly. I cast a furtive glance at the ma'mur and saw his eyes goggling, but he soon pulled himself together: 'And who might the sailor be?' he asked.

The man was silent. As the silence deepened, I had a feeling — I know not whether it was well founded or pure imagination — that the fellow had understood our thoughts perfectly from the very first.

16 October

We could get nothing out of Shaikh Asfur; nor could we arrest him, for he had done nothing punishable by law; so we let him go. It occurred to us that we might set an informer after him in an effort to find out the place where the girl was hidden. But where could we get a secret informer unknown to Shaikh Asfur? He knew all the police employees intimately; he had gone out on cases with them hundreds of

times and stayed up all night in their company, eating and drinking, singing and roistering. In fact, he had often shown them where arms were hidden and gone with them to track the criminals down. He was almost regarded by the police as one of the family. So we let him go on his way in peace and the enraged ma'mur had to content himself with escorting him to the door with a punch in the neck to relieve his own feelings. We each went off to our respective affairs: the ma'mur to his club and I to my house, where I took off my clothes and enjoyed an hour of solitude, in which I could take out my diary and insert this record, for which I can find no other audience in this village. The pen is a great boon to those like us whose destiny is solitude. But the pen, like the horse, is liable to shoot off on its own in gay flight, or to heave or start on its hind legs, refusing to advance, as if there were a serpent rearing its head in the way. And my pen would sometimes quiver in my hand and leap about, refusing to obey me, as if something frightened it away from the visionary pastures where it sought to roam. Glancing at my cupboard, I saw a black mouse on top of it, standing there and chewing away at the wood. I began to glare at it to make it go away; but it remained. Time passed and the mouse and I remained as we were, each of us, no doubt, occupied with the business in hand. The mouse was clearly unaware of my existence though I was well aware of the mouse. Its visit at that particular time dispelled my cares and I began to watch it rubbing its head and mouth with its little paws.I was giving much thought to this creature — which gave no thought to me. Herein lay the entire difference between me and it. Soon I forgot about this small carpenter, with its effective little saw, and went to bed with my book, first wrapping the mosquito net around me, tying its edges tight enough to be safe from the attentions of my visitor if it should feel an impulse to play with my bare feet. For I see no purpose in mouse-traps, as it is too much trouble to prepare them and await the result. There is no greater

nuisance than to be called to waste time in that expectation; even when the victim appears, it eludes us and runs all round, so that by the time it eventually succumbs we are utterly exhausted. Besides, think how many mice we catch, and they still frequent our society. So we might as well let them come and go at will with good grace and devote our attention to our own affairs. Heaven alone knows, I had enough cares without worrying about this cheap stick of white furniture so battered by constant moving from one village to another. What harm could come to it from the playful attentions of those tiny teeth?

I went to sleep shortly after nightfall for on the following day there was to be a session of the court, presided over by our brisk judge, and I had instructed my assistant to be present, with myself by his side, to train him in court procedure and the formalities which are observed on these occasions. When morning came, I went to the court, where I found my assistant in the conference room holding under his arm the envelope containing his official sash. He was waiting for the judge, who soon arrived from his journey on the Cairo train, followed by Sha'ban the court usher. They were striding along briskly, and the judge was pulling money out of his pocket and handing it to Sha'ban: 'It must be real country meat, ribbed cutlets. And be careful about the eggs, Sha'ban Effendi; and butter and cheese as you always get. Pack it all nicely in the basket, and wait for me at the station for the 11 o'clock train, as usual. You go off to the market — the attendant will do your work for you.'

The usher went off briskly and the judge came in, greeting us hurriedly: 'I think we'll go in now.' He clapped his hands: 'Usher, call the court to order. Hurry up!'

He threw his white linen travelling coat on a chair, produced his red sash from his case and donned it instantly. The office-boy brought some coffee, which the judge swallowed in a couple of gulps, without sitting down. He then charged into the court room, with us on his heels.

70

'Court in session!' yelled the usher.

The judge examined the list of cases. 'Misdemeanours! Muhammad Abd al-Rahim al-Danaf... Failed to remove the cotton-worm. Absent—fifty piastres fine. Tuhami al-Sayyid Unaiba... Failed to bring his son for inoculation. Absent — fifty piastres. Mahmud Muhammad Qindil... In possession of a rifle without a permit. Absent — fifty piastres and gun confiscated... Absent — fifty piastres... Absent — fifty piastres...'

The judge shot out his sentences like arrows. Nothing gave him pause. The usher only had time to call out each name once if he wished to keep up with the judge. If someone did not hear his name, he was considered absent and sentenced *in absentia*. If someone happened to hear his case called, he would come rushing forward, only to be anticipated by the judge: 'You, sir, let your sheep graze in your neighbour's pasture.'

'The fact is, your honour...'

'I've no time to listen to stories. Defendant present. Fifty piastres... Abd al-Rahman Ibrahim Abu Ahmad', etc, etc.

The misdemeanours were dealt with in a flash. Next came the turn of the felonies, which involve the hearing of witnesses and the submissions of counsel, and thus require a certain amount of deliberation. The judge produced his watch and put it down in front of him. 'Hurry up with the first case!' he shouted at the usher.

'Salim Abd al-Majid Shaqraf!' called the usher.

The judge glanced at the case-list, ascertained the charge and turned to the defendant. Before the man had crossed the threshold of the courtroom he shouted to him, 'Did you hit the woman? Yes or no? Tell me at once!'

'Your honour, does a gentleman strike a woman?'

'No philosophy here! One word — that's all. Did you hit her, yes or no?'

'No.'

The judge addressed the usher: 'Pleads not guilty. Fetch the witness.'

71

The woman who had been struck hobbled up in her long black dress. The judge yelled at her without waiting for her to come in, 'Did he hit you?'

'The point is, your honour, God bless you...'

'There's no point. Did he hit you or did he not? One word is enough!'

'He hit me.'

'That's enough. The court dispenses with further witnesses. What have you got to say, defendant?'

The man coughed and began a speech of defence. The judge ignored him, being busy writing the evidence and judgment in the case-list with a pencil. When he had finished, he lifted his head and pronounced his sentence without looking at the defendant or waiting to hear the remainder of his defence: 'Month with hard labour. Next case...'

'Your honour! I've still got witnesses. I didn't strike her at all. It's an injustice. Listen, everybody, it's unjust!'

'Be quiet! Take him away, constable!'

The man was removed and the next case was called. A decrepit bent-backed man with a white beard came forward, hobbling on a stick. The judge pounced on him with a question: 'You expended reserved wheat?'

'It was my wheat, your honour, and I ate it with my family.'

'Pleads guilty. One month with hard labour!'

'A month! Do you hear, Muslims! My own wheat, my own crop, my own property...!'

The policeman dragged him away. As he went, he stared at those in court with goggling eyes as though he could not believe that he had heard the sentence aright. Surely his ears must have deceived him and the spectators must have heard the truth. For he had stolen no man's wheat. It is true that the usher had visited him and 'reserved' his wheat, appointing him as its trustee until such time as he paid the government tax. But the pangs of hunger had seized him violently — him and his family; so he had eaten his own wheat. But who

72

could possibly regard him as a thief on that account and punish him for stealing? It was impossible for this old fellow to understand a law which called him a thief for eating his own harvest, sown by his own hands. These were crimes invented by the law to protect the money of the government or of private creditors; but they were not natural crimes in the eyes of the poor farmer, whose simple instinct could not find any sin in them. He knows well enough that assault is a crime, and murder is a crime, and theft is a crime; for all these involve an obvious aggression against somebody else and reveal clear and evident moral turpitude. But 'expending reserved property' — this was something whose principle and definition he could not grasp. For him it was purely a formal, legalistic crime, whose impact he must go on enduring without believing in it at all.

So the old man resigned himself to his Creator; and he was taken into custody, muttering, 'There is no power and no might save in God!' The next case was called. Before the usher could pronounce the name of the accused the judge had weighed the file in his hand and found it heavy with the testimony of many witnesses. He glanced at his watch and then looked at the advocate's bench, where he saw no counsel for the accused. I understood that he intended to adjourn the case, and my expectations proved correct; for he turned to the Prosecution and asked, 'Does the Prosecution wish for an adjournment?'

My assistant turned to me in embarrassment. I replied hastily, 'On the contrary, sir. The Prosecution objects to any adjournment.'

The judge smothered his disapproval and mumbled, 'Oh, well, let us hear it. Call the witnesses.'

Suddenly, however, he remembered that this case was an appeal against a previous sentence pronounced *in absentia*, and that such an appeal should be presented within three days. He briskly read out the relevant dates and immediately addressed the accused with a sigh of relief: 'The case is rejected

on technical grounds as the appeal was presented too late!'

The wretched peasant understood nothing of this pronouncement. 'So what do I do, your honour?'

'The previous sentence of imprisonment must be carried out. Take him into custody, constable!'

'But it's unjust imprisonment, your honour. I've been wronged! No judge has heard my case, no court has asked me any questions to this very day!'

'Be quiet. Your appeal was presented too late!'

'So what?'

'The law provides that you are limited to three days.'

'But — your honour — I'm a poor man. I can't read or write. Who is there to explain the law to me and read out the dates?'

'It seems that I've been too patient with you. You silly animal, you are supposed to know the law. Take him into custody, constable.'

The man was put among the prisoners; as he went, he looked to left and right to see if he was the only one to whom the whole process was incomprehensible. And I began to ponder for a moment on the misery of this creature who was 'presumed to understand' the Napoleonic code.

Finally, the session came to an end. The judge leapt up and rushed back to the conference room, hastily removing his sash. There were only seven minutes to go before the departure of the return train; but the judge was quite accustomed to last-minute embarkations and, for all his haste, lost nothing of his inner certainty and quiet confidence. He seized his white travelling coat, draped it over his arm, bade us farewell and went off to the station at a trot.

Suddenly the clerk of the court rushed in with some files, closely followed by a policeman dragging a prisoner. 'Has the judge gone?' he panted. 'We've got an appeal against imprisonment to be submitted to his honour.'

'Catch the judge at the station before he leaves,' I replied.

The clerk screamed at the policeman, 'Bring the prisoner,

sergeant, and come along to the station.'

Everybody hurried off — the clerk, the sergeant, and the prisoner running behind his guard, tied on to a chain, as though he were a dog. They all rushed after the trotting judge. This was a familiar spectacle to the villagers on the days of these sessions, for late appeals and renewals of imprisonment orders were always examined and signed in the station buffet two minutes before the departure of the train. The train would start moving while the judge had one foot on the platform and the other in the rear compartment, and pronounced judgment: 'Appeal rejected and imprisonment of defendant to continue.'

The clerk would record this judgment on the marble table of the buffet, while the judge received the basket of eggs, butter and meat from Sha'ban, who came sprinting behind the moving train, shouting at the top of his voice, 'Good meat, sir — ribs and kidneys!'

After the session I went to the office with my assistant, whose expression was rather glum. He had imagined that in every case the Prosecution would submit its views on the charge. For this contingency he had prepared long depositions, written in a beautiful hand, on ruled foolscap sheets. And here he was taking them out of the court unopened — just as he had brought them in — while the judgments had been shot out simply and briskly with the speed of an express train. Justice had run its normal course in the twinkling of an eye without any need of the detailed analysis, commentary, testimony and corroboration which he had spent nights in cramming into those papers.

At last I was alone in my office. The Head of the Criminal Section came in with the mail. He opened the envelopes before me, as he was accustomed to do every morning. When he had opened no more than a couple of letters, we heard a commotion outside the room and a sonorous voice, which I recognized as that of Shaikh Asfur. I sent someone out to

find out what was happening, and was told that the police station had put him under arrest, having made out a vagrancy charge against him. I understood that the ma'mur, still believing that this old man had kidnapped the girl and still boiling with rancour against him, had had recourse to 'administrative measures' to get hold of him. To charge Shakh Asfur with vagrancy was certainly a brilliant idea which could only emanate from the intelligence of the enraged ma'mur. It was true that Shaikh Asfur was nothing but a vagrant, and from that viewpoint was a suitable victim of our legal texts. But the remarkable thing was that the police could ignore him for all those years without giving a thought to his occupation until this very day. I did not admire this device very much, and it did not really satisfy my judicial conscience. For the regulations ought not to be weapons in our hands wherewith we could attack whomsoever we wished whenever we chose. it was clear that the arrest of Shaikh Asfur was an act of pure vindictiveness; the ma'mur, having seen the old man escape from the charge of kidnapping the girl, had plotted and devised another plan from which his victim could not hope to escape. This 'administrative method' was hardly worthy to be followed by judicial officers, and I decided to myself that I would release Asfur. However, I postponed consideration of the case until such time as I was free from the morning's mail which lay before me.

Abd al-Maqsud Effendi presented me with a heavy yellow envelope, which I knew must contain criminal cases sent from head office to be studied and prepared for submission to the criminal court, which was to hold session that month in the capital of our province. I glanced at these cases and found them to contain hundreds of pages; I had no head for such troubles at that moment. There was nothing which made me loathe the work of a public prosecutor more than the task of making submissions in cases of felony. My weak memory found it difficult to grasp all the details which went

to make up a criminal charge so as to be able to set them out afterwards in due order and calm before three glowering judges of appeal, with counsel ready to pounce and an audience judging not according to the essence and core of the case, but according to the skill of gesticulations and attitudes, the resonance of a voice in the court, facility in delivery and violence in desk-thumping. By nature I am fitted to be a hidden observer of people strutting across the stage of life — rather than to be a skilled actor flooded with limelight under the eyes of an audience. For such situations dazzle and unbalance me, so that I lose my memory and am deprived of that inner calm wherewith the deeper issues can best be observed. I therefore had no hesitation in turning these cases over to my assistant. For he is still of an age to be impressed by such situations, and might be well enough qualified to justify me in turning them over to his care. Moreoever, I could give him an opportunity of spending a few days in the capital, in whose bars and cabarets he would find some diversion and relief from the austere solitude of this quiet village. I found these admirable arguments sufficient to persuade me to unload those bulky files on to his shoulders.

The Head of the Criminal Section next handed me another small envelope on which I read the word 'Secret' written in red ink. I assumed it to be a note from the Public Prosecutor, and opened it hurriedly. To my surprise it turned out to be a statement by someone unknown which had been sent directly to the Public Prosecutor in Cairo, and then forwarded to me for necessary action. I unfolded it and read it with minute care and, before reaching its conclusion, was overcome with astonishment. After a moment's silent thought I perused it again and slowly read it line by line:

To His Excellency the Public Prosecutor — Cairo.
May Allah prolong his days...

We hereby inform you that the wife of Kamar al-Dawla

Alwan, who lies wounded at the Government Hospital, died two years ago by strangulation. The village barber, ——— , concealed the murder in consideration of a bribe, and performed the burial without the knowledge of the government. You should ask her husband Alwan and her sister Rim who strangled her. The motive of the murder is known and will not elude your sagacity if you take the trouble to investigate yourself, whereupon you will discover important secrets and clip the wings of evildoers and restore Justice to its place. For Justice is the foundation of authority, and Allah, be He exalted and magnified, hath said in His Holy Book: 'And if ye judge amongst men, then judge ye in righteousness.' Verily the word of Allah is truth.

A Well-doer

I gave much thought to that letter. Who could its anonymous author be? The style betold an Azharite fallen on evil days. The Quranic verse and the signature could only emanate from the type of man who exploits his own little knowledge and the abysmal ignorance of the villagers and lives by writing letters for hire, and spreading discord between families and individuals. But whatever the truth might be, this letter contained statements which deserved investigation. For if it was true, as stated, that the wife of Kamar al-Dawla had been murdered by strangulation, we were confronted by a crime begotten of another crime. We were thus less concerned with the authorship of the letter than with the need for assuring ourselves about the veracity of its accusation. It was therefore necessary to open the grave and exhume the body of the wounded man's wife, and submit it for examination to the government pathologist. My thoughts were concentrated on this point, and I did not trouble my mind about what was said in the letter about Rim and with the possible injury that the accusation might inflict upon her. Everything depended on the result of the exhumation.

78

I hastened to notify the government pathologist by telegram and carried out the necessary formalities of exhumation, including the appointment of watchmen to guard the vicinity of the grave at night so that nobody could do any mischief. I sent for the gravedigger. I had already been in touch with the police station by telephone to inform the ma'mur as soon as I had read the letter. I was told that he was on his way to an important meeting in the governorate under the presidency of the governor himself. His inspector came to see me immediately. 'Naturally, sir, you've read the evening papers,' he said.

'Not at all.'

'There's a ministerial crisis in the country.'

I now understood the cause of the meeting at the governorate and realized that henceforward the members of the administration would have no mind or thought for anything except to predict how the new ministerial wind would blow, so that they might adapt themselves accordingly — as they had done on similar occasions before. This process becomes most conspicuous in the rapid depression of the umdahs and notables who were known to favour the outgoing government and the gentle smile of the new government's adherents. I made no comment to the inspector. As a member of the judiciary I have no right to talk politics. Government and parties come and go, but the law remains. Finally, I turned to him and said quietly, 'I think that you can deputize for the ma'mur.'

'The circumstances prevent me from leaving the station; but the registrar is at your service.'

I let him go off to his station and ordered the car. I then sat down and waited for the pathologist, who had replied to our telegram with a telephone message, announcing that he would come today. Abd al-Maqsud came in and pointed to the notice-board hanging on the wall to remind me that we had to inspect the station prison. The Legal Department has to carry out this inspection without prior notice at least

twice a month. I paid no heed and told him to remind me again later. He moved off and, after a few steps, returned and winked at me: 'There's a rumour that the new government has been formed and intends to carry out new elections.'

'So what?'

'I mean to say... the point is... before the prison gets too crowded...'

I uttered no word, pretending to be busy turning over the papers of the case in which we were engaged. The Head of the Criminal Section saw that I had no intention of replying and went away with slow, hesitant steps. I called to him and he came back once more. I addressed him with a cunning smile: 'Did the district clerk talk to you on the phone?'

'Of course,' he replied in an instant, 'and the prison registers are filled in and ready. The inspection report is all written up. Everything is in order — all that remains is your honour's signature. The whole matter isn't worth more than a quarter of an hour and we'll have finished with the prison inspection...'

I looked at him furtively. 'Very good, then. "Inspection without notice complete, Abd al-Maqsud Effendi."'

He seemed rather embarrassed and hastened to explain: 'My only concern is your honour's convenience, on the one hand; and not to trouble the station in the present circumstances, on the other...'

'All right, all right!' I closed the subject hastily, for I heard a knock at my door and caught sight of the pathologist, carrying his bag and awaiting permission to enter.

I got up immediately, went to meet him and bade him welcome. I ordered a cup of coffee for him and we made general conversation for a while, during which he informed me briefly of what I had previously learned from Abd al-Maqsud Effendi. The new government had actually taken office and was preparing for new elections. We made no comment on all this, as neither of us knew the opinions of

the other and we both feared to reveal our hidden thoughts. So we discussed the case in hand and I informed the pathologist of the circumstances in a few rapid sentences. We decided to lose no time in going off to the graveyard. We got into the car and moved off, not stopping until we had reached a distant place amongst the fields, where two or three graves lay together in the shade of a few palm-trees. The graves were of mud and clay, and long dirty tombstones were set over them like the heads of scarecrows. We got out of the car and the watchmen hurried to meet us; they had leapt up from their resting places when they caught sight of us and had come out towards us, some of them climbing over the tops of mattresses which had been laid over the grave like a howdah on a camel's back; others jumping over straw mats which had been spread in front of the grave, like monkeys popping out of their mother's lap. I inquired about the registrar, whereupon they pointed to the road amongst the fields, where I saw a young man in uniform trotting along on a grey horse. In an instant we had begun our work. We ordered the gravedigger to open the grave and he got busy with pickaxe and hammer, breaking down the scaffolding which blocked the entrance of the grave.

The doctor asked me if we had summoned one of the dead woman's relatives who could identify the corpse and the shroud. I replied that we knew of no relatives except one who had escaped and vanished. He suggested that we send the registrar into the village to bring one of the neighbours who might have been present at the washing of the corpse or its burial. The registrar duly departed on his mission, while the gravedigger went on hammering and knocking until he had made a wide fissure in the grave. Thereupon he moved away from it, muttering, 'I'm sorry — the entrance is on the other side.'

He took up his tools, went over to the opposite side and began to widen the hole with much knocking and banging.

The pathologist shouted at him, 'What is it —

Tutankhamen's grave, you fool? You get the wrong entrance and you're supposed to be the local gravedigger!'

'Sorry, doctor, but actually it's been closed for a long time.'

He struck a couple more blows, whereupon the entrance of the grave came open. He crawled inside on his hands and knees and emerged holding something, wrapped up in cloth, colourless through age and almost disintegrating in his fingers. He laid this object before us, saying, 'Have a look at this. Is this the woman you're after?'

The doctor uncovered the withered bones, examined them and turned to the gravedigger: 'Go back, you donkey — this is a man's corpse!'

'A man?'

He disappeared inside the grave with the corpse and emerged again with another one, which the doctor, after a brief examination, found to be that of another man. And so it went on: the fellow kept presenting us with corpses as they came to hand; and they were all men. Eventually he burst out in rage, 'Where, in God's name, have all the women gone?'

'In brief, my friend,' said the doctor, quietly, 'you've got the wrong grave. Open the next one!'

The gravedigger took his tools and followed the pathologist's direction, while the watchman closed the first grave, whispering, 'Well, well, we were on the wrong track.'

The next grave was opened. As soon as the gravedigger had vanished inside it, the registrar came up, followed by a woman who hid her face with a corner of her black veil as she wailed aloud: 'Oh, you who were the light of the village...'

The registrar silenced her with a curse: 'Keep quiet, you old hag!'

The pathologist approached the woman and spoke to her. He discovered that she was a neighbour of the dead woman and had been present at her funeral.

'Listen, my good woman, did they put her in her shroud in your presence?'

She sighed deeply before replying. 'I was there, sir. God protect you — I was beating my face and howling like a babe...'

'We're not interested in what you were doing. How many sheets did they put her in?'

'Three shrouds — touch wood — one of linen, one of kashmir and one of green silk.'

The gravedigger emerged, dragging a corpse. The pathologist examined the shroud, whose colours had faded through age, except for a trace of greenness at the edges which testified to the original colour. He ordered the corpse to be laid on two wooden boards which were quickly set up as a sort of operating table in the shade of an acacia tree. He ordered everybody to move away and the registrar lifted his long stick and dispersed the crowd with a yell: 'Get back there, further, further!'

The pathologist carefully undid the shroud. As the skeleton came to view, I heard a whisper and shuffle behind me and, turning round, saw the driver vanishing behind a tree trunk. He was as pale as a ghost and his eyes protruded as though he could not contain himself at this gruesome spectacle. 'There is no power or device except in Allah! Verily we are unto Allah, and unto Him shall we return!'

The pathologist cursed him and ordered him away, and I too yelled at him; whereupon he went off at a distance to the car and crept inside it. I reflected for a moment, wondering what had agitated him so. Was it the sight of the remains themselves, or the thought of a dead woman lying there, or the nature of all human destiny which he saw visibly before him? Why, then, did the sight of corpses and bones no longer have the same effect on people like me and the pathologist; or even the gravedigger and his watchman? I suppose that these corpses and bones have lost their significance for us, and mean no more to us than pieces of

wood and shreds of timber and lumps of mud and clay. We turn them over with our hands so often in the course of the daily round that they become stripped of their symbolism which is all their strength.

For what remains of all those sacred, awesome things which have such prestige in our mortal lives when we remove their symbolism so that nought remains before our casual, heedless gaze except a thing of gross matter — stone or block of wood of no meaning and no worth? What, after all, is the fate of life and what is its value when its symbol departs — that symbol which exists and yet has no existence, which is at once nothing and everything in human life? This nothing on which we build our lives is all that we possess of higher vision, to distinguish us from the lower animals.

The pathologist cut in on my reflections — with the surgical scissors with which he was examining the corpse. His hands were swathed in transparent rubber gloves. 'This one is definitely a woman.'

He went on working for a while, and then spoke again: 'The ribs are whole, and the skull. But the neck vertebrae...'

I looked carefully, for the neck vertebrae are an eloquent token of crime. If they are broken, it means that strangulation may have taken place. In fact, our only concern in exhuming the corpse was to examine those bones and see if they were sound or not.

The pathologist gave me no time to ask him the result, for he gave a sudden shout as he pointed to the bones between his fingers: 'Broken!'

The single word was sufficient to make the position clear. So the anonymous report was true! What could we now expect? I told the pathologist that we had finished the exhumation, and prepared to hurry back and take the necessary steps to unearth the secret of our new discovery. No doubt this new mystery was the key to the old.

The pathologist had finished with the body, and the gravedigger restored it to its resting-place and buried it as

84

before. I stood in silence, wondering who this woman's murderer could be. Was it the wounded husband? What could be his motive? And the sister Rim — what did she have to do with the affair? Could she have any knowledge of this crime? Where was Rim? It was now of the utmost importance that she should attend the inquiry today. But how could we find her? Shaikh Asfur knew her whereabouts, or could at least help us to look for her. There was nothing for it but to make him the starting-point for our new line of inquiry. I would have to persuade him with my own methods, which were very different from the rather violent usages of official investigation. He was the sort of fellow who could only be influenced by patient resource. For instance, I might persuade him that I could get Rim to marry him. The idea pleased me and I resolved to carry it out.

We rode back in the car. On our way we passed the village and heard women's voices uplifted in grief and wailing, issuing from the umdah's house. I stood up in the car and leaned out, inquiring, 'Is the umdah dead?'

I beheld a spectacle which I could not understand at first. There was the head ghafir and his deputy, and some others, carrying an object in their hands. Around them were crowds of men, women and boys, reciting prayers and verses, while the women ululated as they do at joyful celebrations and beat on tambourines. I looked closely to find out what they were carrying and the pathologist followed my gaze in stupefaction. We saw that it was an official telephone! The doctor exclaimed in astonishment, 'The telephone's got a procession like a bride!'

One of the watchmen passed near us and I beckoned to him. I asked him what the matter was and he replied that an order had been issued that day dismissing the umdah and appointing another in his place — a member of the rival family in the village. We understood the whole situation and the pathologist turned to me with a grin. 'It appears that the umdah's telephone is a kind of royal sceptre.'

He was quite right. The telephone was indeed the symbol of authority and dominion, as well as the means of communication with the government. If it was uprooted from the home of the discharged umdah, that was a symbol of vanished authority. The voice of weeping with which the telephone was escorted from the former umdah's house was a sign of deep disaster. And, like all disasters, it had its opposite aspect of smiling fortune: for the household of the new umdah, which was receiving the incoming telephone with ululations and the beatings of tambourines, it betokened a wealth of happiness and joy. The symbolic telephone of wood and iron played an important role in the life of this peaceful village.

As the car sped along, the pathologist was silent for part of the way. Eventually he turned to me and spoke: 'It seems that the new umdah is one of the clients of our new government.'

'Like all other villages in Egypt today,' I replied, 'this village has two powerful families or more which compete for the umdah's office. Each of them belongs to one of the parties which fight for power. How can you expect the position of the village to be different from that of the country as a whole? The village, after all, is only the state in miniature...'

18 October

As soon as I returned to my office, I sent someone to fetch Shaikh Asfur. He was soon standing before me, silent and downcast. I shot a question at him: 'Do you like the girl, Rim?'

He raised his head and gave me a look which seemed to penetrate my inmost soul. He then looked down again without answering.

'I'm ready to call the marriage registrar and fix a wedding

between you at once,' I said.

He remained unmoved.

'If only she were here now,' I continued.

For all my efforts to cajole him into speech he remained stubbornly silent. Finally he began to hum in a low but clear-toned voice:

> Don't say I didn't warn you,
> But your nature overcame you.
> A dog's tail can't be straightened
> By hanging on a weight.

I lost my temper completely and shouted, 'Shut up, you dog!'

I chased him out briskly, for it was clear that there was nothing to be hoped for from him. I decided to interrogate the barber and, having summoned him, I asked him about the strangled woman and how she was allowed to be buried without the permission of the Legal Officer. He replied immediately, 'By your honour, sir, I don't know if she was strangled or mangled. The doctor ordered her to be buried in the ordinary way.'

'Without signing an examination certificate?'

'Sir, if we had to wait till we had examined every dead body, it would be time for us to die ourselves.'

'In short, nobody examined her and nobody looked at her.'

'The usual practice, sir, is for the barbers in the districts to inform the medical inspector by phone. He sits in his office and asks in every case for the cause of death. We answer on the phone, "Doctor, she died as the Lord hath willed." He says, "Bury her then, bury her, bury her"...'

There seemed little use in interrogating this barber. I know these barbers better than most people. Their only concern is to get five piastres from the relatives of the deceased and obtain for them the necessary permission to carry out the burial without ever looking a corpse in the face or going to

the house of the dead. They are mere burial brokers. Even assuming that an occasional one is honest and conscientious enough to go to examine the corpse, what can an ignorant fellow like that discover? He sees a man or woman, recently dead, with no visible wounds. How can he possibly know that there is something suspicious about the manner of death? This whole system of barbers attached to the Health Department — a system unknown to any country in the world — is itself the source of evil. It is very similar to our midwifery system. I shall never forget what a doctor from the central hospital told me once. He had been called out to a case of childbirth in some provincial village and hurried off, only to find the sick woman prostrate on her back, with the arm of the baby protruding from her body. At her side was an old woman with red hair and lips — Sitt Hindiah, the midwife. He learnt that the woman had been in this state for three days, with the arm protruding from her. He asked the midwife why she had waited all that time without calling the doctor. She replied, 'We were awaiting God's secret bounty. We said to ourselves: "May God deliver her safely."' The doctor had then placed his hand in the womb and found it stuffed with straw. The woman's uterus was perforated and she was moribund, beyond all hope. The baby had been dead for two days. Looking around, he had observed a pile of filthy straw at the woman's feet, and had asked the 'midwife', Sitt Hindiah, for an explanation. 'Well, doctor,' she said, 'when I put my hand in to get the child out, I found the womb slippery, so I said to myself, "I'd better rub my hand with a bit of straw."' She extended her hand to the doctor, who observed that it was filthy with straw from which her long black nails protruded. 'These midwives deliver a woman of a child as though she were a buffalo,' said the doctor. The sick woman and her baby had both died, and all that the Department of Health had done was to withdraw this 'midwife's' licence. It had not changed the system, though it knew perfectly well that thousands of

babies died in this way every year.

So, as I contemplated the barber, I realized that human life has no value in Egypt; for those who are supposed to care about it care very little.

I dismissed the man, and decided that the best course in a case of this sort was for me to find out who had sent the anonymous message. After a moment's thought it occurred to me that I might show the handwriting to the qadi, who could try to identify it for me from amongst his court officials and advocates. Perhaps he himself had come across this handwriting somewhere. Since I was convinced that the writer of the letter was an Azharite, it was reasonable to search in the religious courts.

I quickly summoned Abd al-Maqsud Effendi, the Head of the Criminal Section, who was a close friend of the qadi, and made him accompany me without further ado. We were soon in the court building asking for the qadi. We were shown to a room where a pair of wooden clogs stood outside the door. Abd al-Maqsud Effendi whispered in my ear that his reverence was doubtless making his ablutions for the noon prayer; and in a few sentences he described the extent of the qadi's piety and spirituality. We knocked at the door and went in.

We saw the qadi, divested of his cloak and turban, sitting on a prayer mat holding a plate of dates culled from a palm-tree which we had seen sprouting in the yard. When he saw us, he rose with a greeting and beckoned us to some chairs. He then ordered us some ginger beer while Abd al-Maqsud decided to relieve me of the task of opening the conversation. Turning to the qadi, he said, 'The Legal Officer has a request to make, sir…'

The qadi replied quickly with a trace of anxiety, 'May it be for good with God's blessing. Is it a personal request or…?'

His demeanour and anxiety reminded me of a story which the ma'mur had told me one day. The governor had suggested that the appearance of the district might be

improved and the interests of hygiene served by building a recreation park in the centre of the village. Some of the notables contributed what they could; and the qadi got to hear of the scheme. He then went to the ma'mur and decried the whole project, suggesting that, instead of a park, a mosque should be erected for the service of God. In support of this proposal he exhorted the citizens to piety and repentance, whereupon the cunning ma'mur acquiesced in his demand and became very enthusiatic over the plan. 'Of course,' he said, 'we shall have to put the mosque proposal to his excellency the governor and I'm sure that he'll agree in advance. Moreover — just to delight his excellency's heart — we'll put your reverence's name at the head of the donors' list as contributing a sum of five pounds.'

The ma'mur went on to relate how, as soon as he pronounced that sum, the qadi's face grew pale. He could think of nothing to say and could not withdraw the proposal. He showed signs of the greatest anxiety. This was exactly what the ma'mur expected, despite what he knew of the qadi's affluence and comfortable circumstances. For there were precious few signs of affluence in his daily life. He lived in a couple of rooms and was content with a diet of a little cheese, a couple of radishes and a few dates. Once the ma'mur had visited him during the Great Feast, and found that his 'reception room' consisted of a couple of wooden stools covered by a dirty sheepskin and separated by a straw mat. He would hoard his ample salary except for two or three pounds which made up his monthly expenses; and at the end of the year he would invest his hoard in the purchase of house-property and land. He declined to put his money in a bank in case its total value became known; and nobody ever discovered where he buried it from the beginning of the year to the end.

The ma'mur went on to tell how the qadi turned up hurriedly in the early hours of the following morning, looking as though he had not slept all night. 'Did you tell

the governor about the mosque scheme?' he asked tremulously. 'Of course,' replied the ma'mur, suppressing a smile, 'and later today I'll be meeting with his excellency.' Thereupon the qadi swiftly took on an ingratiating demeanour and, leaning over to the ma'mur, whispered into his ear, 'Just one thing. The question of the five pounds...'

'What about it?'

'There's no need to mention it...'

This incident suddenly recurred to my mind when the qadi said rather anxiously, 'A personal request?' For I had read his thoughts; he was obviously afraid that we were coming to ask for some donation; so I hastily restored his serenity by informing him that we had come on a matter connected with our official positions.

We extracted the mysterious letter from our bunch of papers and put it before him, explaining what we required.

'A simple matter,' he said, with evident relief. 'First let's have a drink. Then we'll consider the matter of the letter.'

He clapped his hands and shouted, 'Shaikh Husain. Bring the tray!' After a brief silence he greeted us again: 'Welcome, welcome! This is a great honour...'

Abd al-Maqsud Effendi now decided to show me how intimate he was with the qadi. He pointed to the dignitary and turned to me, saying, 'His reverence is one of our profoundest scholars.'

He then addressed the qadi: 'Sir, I shall never forget the day of the lecture when you went for that young schoolmaster...'

The qadi interrupted him with pious imprecations: 'God put him to shame! I cannot endure ignorance and blasphemy. Just imagine' — and here he turned to me in appeal — 'imagine this young man, a teacher of geography in a secondary school, giving a public lecture about some Christian scientist called Shentoon, who claims he knows the exact weight of the heavens and the earth. I seek forgiveness of mighty Allah...'

I pondered a little over the name which the qadi had pronounced and finally reached the conclusion that he meant the mathematician Einstein. I was intrigued to know the sequel; no doubt it had been a struggle between two mighty intellects — the sort of clash which I always like to observe and weigh up.

'Were you at the lecture, sir?' I asked, with considerable interest.

'I was there. Allah is supreme over past and future!'

'And what happened?'

'What happened, my friend, is that this teacher got up in the presence of the governor, the senior officials and the notables, and said that this infidel scientist had discovered what nobody in modern or ancient times had ever discovered before. Whereupon I got up and shouted, "It's a lie, my schoolmaster friend. Mighty Allah has said in His Holy Book: We have omitted nothing in this Book." The audience ordered me to be silent and I obeyed in deference to the governor's presence. Otherwise, by the Lord of the Holy Rock, I should not have held my peace. The speaker went on talking nonsense for a time, and eventually said that this infidel scholar had managed by algebraic equations to calculate the weight of the heavens and the earth. I could no longer restrain my anger and I got up and declared, "Very well, sir. Very well. First of all, kindly inform us if this scientist Shentoon measured the heavens and the earth with or without the Throne?" The teacher was puzzled and turned to me, asking, "Which Throne?" Whereupon I recited the holy verse of the Quran: His Throne comprehends the Heavens and the Earth, adding, "Answer me, my dear mendacious schoolteacher! This is the point and essence of the matter. Was the weight calculated with or without the Throne?"'

I suppressed my laughter and inquired with a show of gravity, 'And what happened in the end?'

'In the end? Nothing happened. The lecturer couldn't

92

answer. He just expostulated and withdrew; the audience was in tumult and uproar broke loose. The governor was angry with me and considered that his dignity had been insulted. The people forgot about the lecture, which was the main issue, and turned their attention to my insult to the governor, which was a secondary issue. They all thronged round me, demanding that I apologize, which I did. God be praised! But, nevertheless, I've felt ever since that day that his excellency the governor regards me with some disfavour.'

He was silent for a moment, and then he inquired in a very different tone, 'I suppose that, in view of today's political situation, the new government will make changes and revisions amongst the governors of provinces and officials, as usual?'

Before I could answer, the attendant came in. He was half a shaikh, in that he wore an ecclesiastical turban with an ordinary filthy galabieh, and his feet were bare. He proffered two cups of different pattern — one with a broken handle — and I drank cautiously, staring into the interior of the cup, for I feared that I should find a grasshopper instead of sugar.

Having finished with general conversation and refreshments, we got down to business. The qadi sent for various papers in his officials' handwriting and we compared them with the writing of the letter; but we found none similar. We showed the letter to the people in the court, in case somebody would recognize the owner of the writing. This, too, was in vain. So we left the court with nothing achieved and went on our way to the office of the Legal Department.

'Let's drop in and inspect the prison and be done with it,' suggested Abd al-Maqsud.

I raised no objection and we made for the police station, where we found that the ma'mur had assembled some of the umdahs in his room and had begun expounding the new point of view and issuing instructions with the same

93

enthusiasm as when the previous government had first taken office. As soon as he saw me and guessed the object of my visit, he hurried to meet me and gave me a seat in the middle of the room. He then broke up the meeting, accompanying the umdahs to the door with a parting word of exhortation: 'See to it, umdahs. The government candidate in the election must win! I shall stand aside and give you a free hand. Understand?!'

'We understand, sir,' they replied with one voice.

One of them hesitated: 'Well, sir, there's a group of tough fellows with great influence from the other big family...'

The ma'mur nudged him violently. 'Tough fellows, eh? Leave them to me. It's all right!'

They went out together and the ma'mur came back, sighing happily and speaking in a weary voice: 'I've had two days and two nights of this nonsense.'

I thought I would frighten him for a joke. I said, 'But, my dear ma'mur, you're well known as a supporter of the previous government.'

'For God's sake, don't say that!' he replied quickly. 'All my life my heart has been with the new government. It's what the heart says that counts. The intention behind the deed is what matters.'

I smiled and said, 'Let's leave politics and talk about our work.'

I informed him of the result of the exhumation and the discovery of the broken bone in the neck. I urged the necessity of looking for the culprit of the new crime of strangulation, and asked for his co-operation in helping us to track down the criminal.

'The police station won't be free for a couple of days for worrying about stranglers and fires,' he replied curtly.

'That's strange. Have you any duty apart from the preservation of order?'

'You mean... you don't understand...?'

'I certainly don't.'

'You imagine that we can forget the elections and worry about murders?'

'Naturally.'

'Our instructions are quite different!'

He turned away and began to toy with some handcuffs and chains hanging on the wall. Abd al-Maqsud winked at me to suggest that I close the subject; he made an effort himself to turn the conversation into different channels. 'May I bring the prison register?' he said to the ma'mur.

I felt that the dignity of my office was being undermined, and I replied heatedly, 'I must inspect the prison and the whole station myself.'

I got up with an air of firm resolve which seemed to perturb the ma'mur. He hesitated for a moment, and then said quietly, 'By all means. The prison is at your disposal. If you don't mind waiting a moment...'

He went out quickly, calling for Corporal Abd al-Nebi. As he vanished, I felt moved to glance through the window overlooking the courtyard. I saw the ma'mur and the corporal rush over to the prison, open it and fetch out a number of people, whose appearance showed them to be well-to-do local residents. I then saw the two of them push all these prisoners into the fodder store and lock the door upon them.

'Come here,' I said to Abd al-Maqsud. 'Come and look for yourself. Is this a prison or a Bastille? The ma'mur has hidden some people in the straw room!'

He replied in a tone of appeal, 'It's a sad time, sir. Politics are supreme in this country. It's no use being too pedantic.'

'You mean that we should leave people in prison for no crime?'

'You know very well that the ma'mur's chief is the Minister of the Interior and the Prime Minister as well. Our chief is only the Minister of Justice. There have been cases where judges and Legal Officers took your attitude towards the administration — and found themselves transferred to Upper Egypt.'

'So we just sign the prison register and keep quiet?'

'Well, sir, we couldn't do better or wiser. Other people, more clever, might be able...'

'Oh, all right! Hurry up and fetch the register.'

I decided that the only course now was to hunt for Rim's suitor. But how were we to find him when we knew nothing of him — not even his name? We could only get the police to bring one of the neighbours who might know the man. And it had better be a woman neighbour. Women are inquisitive and talkative by nature; and all women know the names of suitors and their girls in the neighbourhood. But was I entitled now to trouble the police station with the job of bringing a witness in or looking for a criminal? Politics were all that mattered in the police station at the moment, and I would not find a single watchman to take any notice of me or my business. So I thought of getting in touch with the village directly and asking the police post to send us the woman we required. I ordered my servant to go and ring up. He seized the receiver and proceeded to shout for a quarter of an hour. 'Police post! Police post! Answer me! The Legal Officer is here. Hello! Hello! Police post!'

But the police post was too sleepy to take the trouble of answering. My servant became more and more enraged and began shaking the telephone bell with enough violence to wrench it off. It was one of the station telephones which never connect two callers until both have lost their breath through excessive screaming. Thereafter contact is interrupted about a hundred times while other conversations from other villages and different departments become entangled with one's own. Thus while you're talking about sending a defendant, you hear a voice replying about something to do with the inspection of an irrigation canal — all about opening bridges and the periods for using the canals. And then another voice starts making authoritative demands about recruitment. Today, however, we got no reply at all, although my servant turned the bell handle as

though he were grinding coffee, while he shouted in alternating tones of threat and supplication, 'Hello, police post, I'm calling you! One word only, police post! Oh, damn you, police post! Hello! Answer me — hello!'

I could stand no more, 'I told you to ask for the police post, not to court it like a girl,' I said.

'Sir, it appears that the police post is empty. No clerk, no sergeant — nobody at all!'

'Can it possibly be empty?'

'Election day, sir.'

'And what about our work?'

'Let's ring the umdah's house and ask for the man and woman that we need.'

'All right. Ring him up.'

Finally, we managed to produce the woman 'by express route', just as it was lunch time. I was tired of a routine day's work — forgeries, usury cases, and crimes coming in from the police station — the usual daily 'income'. Most numerous of all were the charges of vagrancy against persons unfriendly to the new government. This was the easiest and most effective weapon the administration possessed: for every notable's son could be charged with 'having no fixed occupation', and could thus be arrested and imprisoned for four days by permission of the Legal Department, to give time for investigation and to obtain his records from Cairo. And where was the Legal Officer today who would refuse the demands of a police station to issue detention orders?

When I had issued enough of these orders to please God and the police station, I went to have lunch. I came back in the afternoon to interrogate the woman. There was endless discussion, from which I could extract no information except that the young suitor was called Husain, and was not a local resident, but a man from a neighbouring village.

'Husain — what, my good woman? There are hundreds of Husains in these parts. What is his family name?'

'I don't know his name, sir. The girl said his name was

Husain, so why should I ask about his family and all the rest of it? I'm a poor simple woman, as you see; I don't hold with a lot of chatter. All my life round here I've kept away from a lot of talk and questions. What's it got to do with me? You know the saying — "If you get between the onion and the peel, all you'll get is a nasty smell," as they say...'

'Oh, shut up, you're making my brain tired, and all for nothing. May God worry the head of whoever sent you here. Look — if we produce the young man, would you know him?'

'Would I know him, sir? Would I know him? Bless my soul! I should hope so — I'd be quite blind if I couldn't. Saving your presence, sir, do I look as if...'

'That will do. You're a woman, thank God, who doesn't like to talk much, and...'

'Talk much? Of course not, by your life and honour. I've kept away from that ever since...'

'All right — that's enough.'

I sent for my servant and told him to take the woman out and make her sit in the hall next to him and wait until she was sent for. I also instructed him to get in touch with the village where the young man lived and ask them to produce all the young men named Husain whose particulars corresponded with our information. I then sat and waited, reflecting on the doubtful value of this sort of identity parade, so dear to the law. I haven't much faith in the intuition of these women. I can still remember a murder case in which we brought the murdered man's wife and paraded the suspect amongst a crowd of other people whom we fetched at random from a session of the civil court which was in progress that morning. Amongst these people was an unlucky fellow who had come to court with documents proving his part-possession of a buffalo, and was awaiting a judgment of his claim against his rival. He now found himself pushed in amongst the people taken from the court and made to stand in a long row in the office of the Legal

Department. The Legal Officer then produced an ill-favoured old woman and ordered her to identify the murderer amongst those present. She proceeded to scrutinize all their faces, beating her breast the while and uttering curses against the murderer of her husband. She came to the actual murderer and calmly passed him by; and then she arrived opposite the wretched man with the buffalo documents, who had not the slightest connection with the whole matter. Sudddenly she punched him in the chest, almost knocking him down, and let out a shout: 'That's the man. He's the one I'm after!'

The man quivered in astonishment, and then pulled himself together and said, 'But, my good woman, do I know you?'

She took no notice of him and went on shrieking: 'Vengeance! I want my revenge! That's the murderer!'

The man turned to me in urgent appeal: 'Really sir, help me! I have never met or set eyes on this woman before.'

The Legal Officer — I'm ashamed to say that it was I — carried out the routine interrogation, which I knew by heart, and which is a rigid procedure with us. If we fail to carry it out, headquarters consider that we have earned a rebuke — even if the routine has no relevance at all in that particular case. The actual questions are quite absurd and insignificant in themselves, but the law regards them as embarrassing and awkward to criminals.

'Was there any enmity between you and her?'

'None at all, sir. I simply don't know her.'

I paused a little before delivering the question which all Legal Officers and judges ask with complete assurance, as though they have a decisive argument up their sleeves: 'In that case, why should she accuse you?'

'How on earth should I know? It's just a disastrous morning for me — that's all.'

'Take him into custody, constable.'

'Custody? But, sir, I've got a civil action going on downstairs. Please let me go about my business!'

It was to no avail: the man was confined as a precautionary measure. His case was called and, as he was perforce absent, his claim was dismissed. The poor fellow crouched on the asphalt floor, holding his documents and contemplating the harsh fate which had come upon him with no justification or cause.

As I recalled this incident, I warned myself not to attach an exaggerated value to this identity parade. These peasants, whose eyes have been consumed by trachoma since childhood and whose mental faculties have been left to decay under the rule of so many governors of all races, can hardly be relied upon for judgement or discernment of any kind.

The most extraordinary identity parade which I ever conducted was in a case of forgery. The accused was an effendi, and I put him in amongst a lot of people wearing tarbushes, and then produced the peasant who was the victim of the fraud and asked him to identify the man who had wronged him from amongst those present. After scrutinizing their faces for a brief moment, he turned away from the line of people and stood opposite me — the Legal Officer in charge of the inquiry. He stared at me intently for a long time. His eyes showed symptoms of a suspicion — which was soon succeeded by the certainty of having finally hit upon the true culprit. One of the inspectors of our department was visiting us at the time and he expressed a wish to attend an identity parade. I was terrified lest the man should prolong his suspicious scrutiny of myself and give the inspector an unfortunate impression. So I rebuked him and ordered him to look at the row of people before him and produce the suspect from their midst. But the fellow kept on passing along the row and coming back to fix his gaze upon me, examining me from top to toe with an air of profound suspicion. I shall never forget how agitated I was that day. 'May God help these people standing in a row,' I thought to myself. My only resource was to bring the parade to a summary conclusion.

'Victim fails to recognize anyone,' I mumbled hastily, ordering the people to depart. Even as the man went out, he kept looking at me furtively.

No — these procedures which we follow in legal work in accordance with up-to-date regulations really ought to take account of the intelligence of these people and the extent of their mental attainments. The only alternative, of course, is to raise their mentality to the level of our laws!

The people we had sent for came in and we made them stand in a long line. We then admitted the woman.

'In the name of Allah, the merciful and compassionate,' she exclaimed as she stepped forward.

I gave her no time for chattering. 'Just one word, and that's all I want from you,' I said, harshly. 'Which of these people is the girl's suitor?'

She approached the nearest man and looked at him with bleary eyes, rather like those short-sighted public letter-writers who examine their texts by raising them till they touch their noses. She then addressed the man in a low voice, which was not intended for my hearing: 'Tell me, son, isn't your name Husain?'

I immediately saw how much the woman knew of the matter for which she had been deputed. I shouted at her angrily, 'All the fellows in front of you are called Husain!'

'No — really?' she said in a voice of real perplexity. She turned to the second man and asked, 'Where do you come from, son?'

'From Embabeh, ma'am,' he replied.

'That's the village for donkeys,' she snapped back with an air of gravity. 'I once remember my dear old man buying a donkey there...'

I could stand no more. 'Get out, you depraved woman!' I yelled. 'You shameless creature, you hussy! You've wasted our time — a whole day gone! To hell with these witnesses!'

I must have spoken in genuine rage, for I am not accustomed to swearing. But there was this woman who

had given me to understand that she had seen the suitor with her very eyes and would know him if he stood before her; and now it was plain that she knew nothing except his name. And how could we even know if this name 'Husain' was really his? It may have been nothing but the random invention of this garrulous woman.

I asked the other people present about Rim's suitor, but I found no one who understood what I was driving at or who knew anything about the whole subject. So I let them all go. As soon as I was alone, deep in contemplation of our next step, the door opened and my assistant came in. He had returned from the city, where he had gone to make depositions about some cases which I had turned over to him. I saw that his countenance was bright and gay. He greeted me first: 'Big cities are the place to be,' he said. 'What a shame that I had to hurry back to this hellish village.'

'Did you get some acquittals?'

'I stayed at the best hotel and paid twice the amount of my travelling grant.'

'Please answer my questions. What did you do about the cases?'

The young man was rather taken aback. He had not expected to hear me talking about serious business from the very first moment. Actually I should have been more gentle and courteous to him, but this case had wearied my nerves. I confess that a tinge of subconscious jealousy may have stirred in me when I saw this young fellow returning in such a bright mood from the paradise which he was describing, while I was chained to my work and submerged in responsible affairs which seemed never to halt or come to an end. Nevertheless, I was conscious of my own harsh abruptness and would have liked to smile and talk about something unofficial; but the occasion had passed and my assistant proceeded to talk to me about the case in which he had made his submission.

It transpired that the defendant had been sentenced to penal

servitude for life for having killed a man for five pounds. The murderer was a bedu from the Sudan, a great tough fellow who had embraced assassination as a profession. A certain peasant had contracted with him to murder a personal enemy and had signed an agreement setting out the price of this particular 'life'. The assassin had departed with his rifle, with the air of a musician carrying his violin, and had stood under the window of the mosque. In due time the somewhat expensive 'life' entered, made his obeisance and ablutions and began to pray. Thereupon the assassin in ambush dispatched a whistling missile from his fiendish weapon. One shot was enough: for this is a trade which needs a steady hand — like that of a skilful carpenter who only needs to hit a nail once, with no danger of a false or crooked stroke to prevent him from striking the wood plumb in the middle. So it was here. The blood would have been shed and forgotten as usual and the case would have ended with no conviction — but for a dispute between the buyer and seller. For the murderer delivered the goods — but the buyer contested the price. The assassin had no patience for a 'customer' who was defaulting in payment; and in open court, without any regard for the dignity of the law and its guardians, he shouted, 'Do you expect me to kill him for nothing?' Then turning away from his 'customer', he addressed himself to the Bench: 'Gentlemen, bear witness to this dishonourable conduct! I really deserve to be hanged for not having demanded payment in advance. It's this credit system that ruins business!'

My assistant and I laughed over this episode and I expounded my view on this 'trade' of hired assassination so familiar to village life. The Egyptian peasant often has recourse to a professional when he wants some killing done, just as our ancient kings used to employ mercenary soldiers. The cause may lie in some deficiency of character from which the peasant suffers, in addition to his many bodily, mental and social ills. On the other hand, it may be sheer incapacity

and diffidence arising from a long tradition of slavish work at agriculture, leaving the chivalrous and martial qualities to the invaders — most recently, the Arabs and Turks. It is noteworthy that the most celebrated professional assassins in the villages are of foreign blood. Perhaps the reason is that the peasant is a peace-loving fellow and has scruples against shedding blood with the very hand that plants the seed and reaps the harvest. I just don't know — the matter needs special research — and all that we who are in touch with these questions can do is not to pass them over unheeding.

I pointed out to my assistant that our profession was full of material for study and observation, so that as long as he lived he ought not to go about with his eyes closed. A Legal Officer is a little king in his own tiny sphere; if he understands everything that goes on in his kingdom, observes everything, studies men and their natures and instincts, he should be well equipped thereafter to understand the larger kingdom which is his own country, or even the wide world of humanity itself. But how many people in the Legal Department or on the Bench know how to observe things? Power of observation is a great bounty not vouchsafed to all men. My assistant listened attentively to this discourse, for he is a shrewd fellow. After a moment's silence he looked up and told me that he had observed something in the Criminal Court which had arrested his attention. He had noticed that the judges of appeal first pronounced their decision and then proceeded to record their reasons. Logic, as he conceived it, required that the order should be reversed. It was a useful observation on his part. Indeed, a candid appeal judge had once told me how he had pronounced sentence in a certain case of serious felony and had gone back to his office at night with all the files and papers relating to the case, in order to write the evidence. His glance had fallen on certain testimonies and expressions in the record of the session on that day and previous occasions; and when he

came to examine the prosecution's case, his calm and measured thought on that peaceful night discerned some considerations which, had he been conscious of them when he pronounced sentence, would have modified, and indeed reversed, his decision. But what use was that now, since judgment had been given and there was no possible way of changing it? He could do nothing. So he made it his concern that night to extract from the papers all the arguments which could support his judgment. Many a long legal argument is written to justify and support a hasty judgment already given, rather than to explain a just verdict and sift the facts.

20 October
This morning I checked the court accounts; for the Legal Department is responsible for supervising them and must carry out an inspection without prior notice at least twice a month. Evidently the words 'without prior notice' are inserted in the regulations and instructions purely in order to provoke curiosity, like announcements on theatre posters. In point of fact, there is never any element of surprise. The custom is for the Legal Officer to forget this duty in the pressure of other work until he is reminded of it by the cashier whom he is meant to 'surprise'. It is he who insists that the Legal Officer should spring an inspection upon him at exactly ten o'clock, just before the cash is handed in to the governorate, with a form countersigned in accordance with regulations. Usually it is the Legal Officer who suddenly finds himself 'without prior notice' presented with a certificate made out in his name, reading, 'We ... the Legal Officer, today carried out a check of the accounts without prior notice and found therein so many banknotes and so much silver and so many valuables and so much in deposits.' This he signs without moving from his chair, saying, 'Take my signature and go away and leave me alone and stop

worrying me.' I myself, however, go over to the cash-box in person and look at it, even though I ultimately sign without troubling to count the cash.

Having accomplished this duty, I looked in at the store on my way to the office, in order to inspect its contents. This is a room like a Woolworth's emporium, with all kinds of firearms, home-made pistols, knives, blades, scythes, pickaxes, hatchets, sticks, poles, felt caps, sandals, galabiehs stained with blood and dirt, jackets pierced with bullets or gunpowder shots — all duly marked with a number, the date of confiscation and the case for which they were seized. I always think that a single glance at a Legal Department store will immediately indicate the character of the village, its way of thinking and the degree of its civilization. I have no doubt, for instance, that the store of the District Attorney of Chicago would be quite innocent of sticks or home-made pistols.

I went up to the office and found the resident judge awaiting me. The attendant had brought him some coffee; as soon as he caught sight of me, he shouted, 'It's all up! The country is in chaos!'

Before I could so much as open my mouth to ask him what he meant, he continued without interruption, 'There's no respect for judgments any more.'

'Why, what's the matter?'

'The matter, my dear sir, is that I gave judgment in a civil case against one of the umdahs friendly to the government and the usher went to execute the judgment — and what do you think happened?'

'What?'

'He was beaten with the knowledge of the umdah — he was given a good hiding and locked up in the telephone box for twenty-four hours!'

'Didn't the police station take the matter up?'

'Not at all. That's just the trouble. There was no case — not even a report. They just laughed at the usher, made him

withdraw his complaint and closed the matter!'

'Well, as long as they've closed it, we needn't worry.'

'Needn't we? I can't be silent on a matter of this kind. This is a flagrant crime! The police are committing a crime...'

'I can see that your honour is longing for the heat of Upper Egypt.'

'What — do you mean that they'd transfer a judge to Upper Egypt just because he wants to stop the police from tampering with...?'

'Oh, they've done it often. Once they transferred a judge to the remotest part of Upper Egypt because he released on appeal a number of people who had demonstrated against the government, even though he was completely impartial and remote from party politics. Now everybody knows that there's a family quarrel between you and the ma'mur. You'll soon find him writing secret reports about you, accusing you of being an enemy of the government, a fomenter of plots and intrigues, a persecutor of government supporters and a danger to the present policy — and so on, in the well-known style...'

'That's a fine thing — the police writing secret reports against judges.'

'It's happened before.'

'So what should I do?'

'Leave it to me. I'll discuss it calmly with the police station and do whatever is necessary...'

'But see to what extent politics in this country plays about with justice, order and ethics! God preserve us. I tell you it's frightening...'

He shook his head sadly and then turned to me again: 'But you're quite right. Imagine that villainous qadi pretending to be a warm friend of the ma'mur, when he has hated him like poison ever since the incident of the chemist shop.'

I pretended to be surprised, though in fact I had often heard the ma'mur, in the course of conversation, telling this

story about the qadi. It appeared that the people and the notables of the village felt a need for a real chemist shop which would enable them to dispense with the shops of the big cities. So they got up a subscription amongst themselves and collected a sum with which they opened a nice clean shop, with all the proper equipment, and appointed a licensed pharmacist — a Syrian called Jabbur. They then discussed a suitable trustee for the finances and administration of the pharmacy. The final choice fell upon his reverence the qadi. For who could better be trusted to look after the properties of Muslims and other contributors in this village than his reverence with his venerable beard and long cloak? The ma'mur agreed to appoint the qadi as the trustee; and his reverence was graciously pleased to assume his duties, which he did by taking up a position every afternoon at the door of the pharmacy, where he would cough, invoke the name of God, bless the Prophet, his companions and followers, and then call out, 'Mister Jabbur! Coffee and nargilah, please!'

A goodly number of his friends and relations would gather round him every day and he would offer them coffee or tea. All these orders, of course, were at the expense of the shop. Before leaving, the qadi would never forget to scrutinize the window exhibits and say to Jabbur, 'Have you some good scented soap? And I may as well take a bottle of eau-de-cologne.'

As soon as he arrived home, the qadi would find the articles which he had admired already there. Sometimes he would sit at the pharmacy door surrounded by his children, whom he would leave to play about until they became hungry or started crying, whereupon he would yell at the pharmacist, 'Mister Jabbur! Give the children some of your peppermint drops!'

On occasions his reverence the trustee would be in need of a little money, whereupon he would address himself to the chemist: 'Give me four florins from the till!'

A chicken seller would pass by and his reverence would

108

purchase a couple of fat birds and call to the chemist inside his shop, 'Pay from the till, Mister Jabbur!'

Eventually Jabbur's patience was exhausted. 'The till, the till! Good Lord, it's nothing but the till,' he yelled one day.

So a dispute flared up between the pharmacist and the 'trustee', and Jabbur swore that he would break the qadi's leg if he ever showed himself near the shop again. He sought the help of the ma'mur, to whom he revealed what had happened to the pharmacy; for it was now on the verge of bankruptcy. Its stock had vanished and its revenue had dwindled, and no prospect of survival remained. Finally, the pharmacist had followed in the footsteps of the revered trustee and had not stopped short of emptying the remainder of the till and articles in stock. The ma'mur, much incensed, had complained to the notables, who had subscribed to the venture: 'We were wrong to believe in his beard and robes!'

Since that day the ma'mur had always abused the qadi, calling him a swindler, while the qadi, for his part, incessantly attacked the ma'mur as a 'card-playing heathen'.

Now, however, politics had endowed the administrative officials with terrible power. The qadi was fearful of his own fate and deemed it prudent to seek immunity by friendship with the ma'mur, whom he had no hesitation in conciliating and flattering.

All this passed through my mind as I sat opposite the judge. I couldn't help saying, as though to myself, 'Peace is all very well. But in the present circumstances, surely there is something called dignity...'

The judge raised his hand in a significant gesture and said, 'Whose dignity, my dear fellow?'

He got up to go and, as he went, he leant over to me and said in a low voice, 'This is in strict confidence. One day a peasant turned up at my house with a sheep which he said was a "present". I said to him, "What present, my man?" He replied, "The present we agreed about to get judgment restoring my wife to me." I understood what he was driving

at and said immediately, "My dear chap, you've got the wrong house — you want the qadi!"'

I evinced no great surprise and kept looking down. The judge was silent for a while and then moved towards the door of my room with a brief gesture of farewell. I sat alone, thinking; and then decided to go to the police station on a sort of private visit to ask the ma'mur about what the judge had told me. I went off, accompanied by my servant, and came to the ma'mur's room. This time again I found him with one of the umdahs, to whom he was talking rather violently. The umdah's demeanour gave no evidence of propriety or dignity: he seemed a rather crude type to me. For umdahs, like chameleons, assume the likeness of the soil wherein they are born. Green soil produces green chameleons and barren soil produces the grey variety; and this grey umdah was obviously from some poor distant region on the boundary of the district near the desert.

I greeted the ma'mur with a smile. 'Always with the umdahs?'

He replied in a tired voice, 'What can I do?'

He gave me a seat and ordered me some coffee. Despite my habit of avoiding him and his club, he respects me and bears me none of the rancour which he harbours against the others. I am always careful with these administrative officials to carry out my orders in a simple fashion, so as to give them no feeling of discomfort.

The ma'mur asked my permission to finish his conversation with the umdah, so as to be free for my affairs. I assented and he turned to the man and shouted at him in threatening tones, 'Now, you look out! It seems that you don't know me any more! By God, I shall have to...'

The umdah interrupted him in beseeching tones: 'I'm just a poor man...'

The ma'mur proceeded with his dire threats: 'You wait! You see if I don't get you into parliament. You can rely on it so long as I'm ma'mur of this district!'

110

'What have I done wrong so as to be sent to parliament?'

The man spoke pleadingly, in evident fright. I laughed in surprised amusement.

'The electoral lists are in his pocket,' said the ma'mur turning to me. 'But he doesn't know what on earth parliament is. And these are the people they call umdahs and appoint to work with us!'

'You can go now,' he said to the umdah.

He crept out wretchedly like a slave or a criminal. I reflected that the humiliation which he endured in the presence of the officials would not just fade away: it would be transmitted in turn to the people of the village which he ruled. The cup of humiliation is handed on from superior to subordinate in the village until it finally reaches the belly of the miserable 'people', who swallow its contents in one huge gulp.

The ma'mur sat beside me, eager to know the reason for my honouring the police station with a visit. I told him that it was simply my longing to see him, whereupon he smiled in a way that expressed his disbelief of this Platonic motive. I did not insist much on my compliment and said to him gravely, 'Have you been informed, sir, that one of the ushers was beaten and locked up while executing his duty?'

'I've heard nothing,' he replied swiftly.

'Was there no report sent in to this station?'

'If there had been, we would have recorded it and made a case of it.'

'Yes, naturally.'

I was silent for a moment. The ma'mur said, after some cogitation, 'Did anyone tell you anything?'

'If anyone had reported it to me, I would have investigated straight away.'

'Naturally. Of course.'

'It seems that it's merely a rumour.'

'By your life, of course, it's only a rumour,' went on the ma'mur. 'It's a rumour issuing from the court to spoil the

reputation of the police. You know very well that the judge is mixed up in it — all he wants is to libel us in any way he can...'

He wanted to pursue this discourse but I quickly closed the subject, so as to avoid being involved in this quarrel between the two of them. It was sufficient for me to have conveyed indirectly to the ma'mur that I was not overlooking the matter and would not hesitate to take steps about it. We both got up together, and I said, jokingly, 'And the elections...?'

'Going fine!'

'Proceeding according to the rules?'

He stared at me closely and responded with a jest: 'Are we mocking each other? Are there any elections anywhere which go "according to the rules"?'

I laughed. 'What I mean is — the semblance of the rules.'

'If that's what you mean, you can set your mind at rest.'

After a brief pause, he said with fierce emphasis, 'Please believe me, I'm a ma'mur with a sense of honour. I'm not the usual sort of ma'mur. I never interfere in elections and never bring pressure on the liberty of the people in elections, and I never say "Vote for this man" and "Vote against that fellow." Never, never, never, I tell you! Nothing of the kind. My principle is — leave folk alone to vote for whomever they want...'

I could not forbear to interrupt him with words of approval: 'That's really wonderful! But isn't it risky for a man in your position to talk like that? I can see that you're a remarkable person, but...'

'Well, that's my method with elections,' he continued. 'Complete freedom. I let people vote as they like — right up to the end of the election. Then I simply take the ballot box and throw it in the river and calmly replace it with the box which we prepare ourselves.'

'A fine thing!' I spoke with mingled surprise and disappointment. I had no wish to comment on what I had

heard. So I shook hands and said goodbye. As I went out, the ma'mur escorted me to the door; and as I passed across the courtyard, I saw a group of ghafirs preparing to mount a lorry. Amongst them was Shaikh Asfur with his green staff. I turned to the ma'mur for an explanation. He pointed to the group of men and said, 'These fellows will keep order when votes are taken.'

'But what has Asfur got to do with the elections?'

'Oh, his songs have a great influence on the fellahin.'

'You mean — he's a sort of propaganda delegate?'

The ma'mur smiled at this remark approvingly. I smiled with him. 'You've even engaged Asfur for political work,' I said.

The ma'mur looked at me cunningly and sighed: 'What can we do?'

This phrase and the accompanying sigh were sufficient to make me feel sorry for this ma'mur and appreciate the delicacy of his position and his responsibility towards his superiors, who demand certain definite results from him, by whatever means they are obtained, so long as he finds them congenial to his ends. If he were to hold back or hesitate, they would crush him without mercy.

As I walked along, I approached Shaikh Asfur and shot a question at him: 'Where has Rim gone to?'

He looked at me askance without deigning to reply. I repeated my question in a gentle, conciliating tone: 'Rim, my dear fellow. Do help us in the matter of Rim.'

He shook his head, brandished his stick and began to chant:

> What's the use of worrying?
> That will never pay.
> You should have finished off the bird
> Before it flew away!

I smiled back at him and pointed to the ma'mur. 'Tell his

113

honour the ma'mur that story. He was the one who had the bird!'

21 October

As soon as I had drunk my morning coffee in my office, a telephone message came in about a poisoning case in the district. A divorced woman had eaten a cake given to her by her former husband and suspicious symptoms had appeared. She was now accusing him of having poisoned her to escape his alimony obligations. It sounded plausible, and certainly called for investigation. On the other hand, I know all about these poisoning cases and what a nuisance they are — especially in the morning. I knew that I would go along and find a woman wallowing in a pool of vomit and excrement, and that if I addressed any question to her I should get a reply not in words but in... Oh God! I took out my handkerchief and spat into it. I thought of giving the case over to my assistant, and actually sent for him. When he came in, I handed him the message. He glanced over it quickly and exclaimed, 'Poisoning! I've never investigated a poisoning case or even been present at one!'

His objection was reasonable enough. Poisoning, of all things. Not even I, an experienced old hand at this game, could possibly investigate these cases without the due forms specified in the Public Prosecutor's instructions. The forms contained certain specific questions which had to be answered; and a copy of the questions and answers had to be sent with a brief report, enclosing specimens of the vomit and excrement, for analysis. In addition to all this we had to remember to cut the nails of the accused and his pockets, which all had to be sent in sealed envelopes for chemical analysis, because traces of poison often remained in the nails and pockets of the poisoner.

I sent for the clerk and ordered him to make the necessary preparations. I also asked for a copy of the form so that I

114

might glance at it and remind myself of its contents. He brought it along, together with the relevant instructions, and I read the following:

PARA. 141 — When sending the envelope to the Medical Section, the Legal Department must simultaneously send to the Public Prosecutor the undermentioned form with all items accurately completed:

1. Date on which case was notified.
2. Name, age and nationality of victim.
3. State of victim's health before the attack.
4. Symptoms which were observed (e.g. vomiting, diarrhoea, pains, thirst, headache, dizziness, loss of powers of articulation, drowsiness, perspiration, paralysis, condition of heart, pulse, respiration).
5. Whether the victim complained of any unusual taste in the mouth when he took food.
6. Whether the victim felt any numbness or tingling in his tongue or limbs.
7. Whether the victim lost consciousness.
8. Whether the victim felt any nervous contractions or shocks.
9. Whether the symptoms appeared suddenly.
10. Whether the victim had ever experienced a similar condition before.
11. The period between the administration of the suspicious substance and the appearance of the first symptoms.

Note — Clear dates and definite times must be recorded for all the above items, i.e. it is *not* sufficient to write, 'Next day at three o'clock' or 'On Monday', but, for example, 'The symptoms began to manifest themselves at 4 p.m. on the 16th of ——— in the year ———. The first thing to be noticed was ———, which was observed at exactly 3 a.m. ———'.

This was all very fine. These were questions which had to be addressed to a wretched victim who didn't know his head from his heels. And the most remarkable thing was that he had to inform us that the symptoms began at precisely ———— o'clock. It wouldn't do merely to say, 'on Tuesday'. Here was a poor creature drowning in the contents of his own stomach, etc, etc..., according to the form; and this peasant or ignorant woman — who had never carried a watch or even set eyes on one — was supposed to inform us that the symptoms were first observed at precisely one minute past three o'clock!

In the end, we went off to flood the poisoned woman with our questions. I took my assistant along, so as to deprive him of his excuse on future occasions. However, as soon as we set out, another telephone message was handed to me by the servant.

'Beginning of a perfect day!' I said.

It was a note from the hospital, informing me of the death of Kamar al-Dawla Alwan.

'The fellow has died before we could get his secret,' I said.

I called for a pen and added at the bottom of the message the usual formula in such cases: 'We require a post mortem.' I sent my assistant to be present at the autopsy and to inform me of its result as soon as it was over. He went off to the hospital while I repaired to the house of the woman who had eaten the cake. Everything was exactly as I had expected. I found the woman surrounded by her neighbours, who hadn't left a single pot or pan or dish in the street: they had fetched them all and put them under the mouth of the prostrate victim, who was writhing in her death convulsions. I indicated to the clerk that he could begin his report and advanced between the pots and pans, which were already full. When I came to the victim, I proceeded to interrogate her. 'Your name, age and nationality?'

There was no answer. Her pale face gave no sign of comprehension. I repeated the question at the top of my

116

voice, and nothing came from her mouth except a long-drawn-out moan, mixed with the noise of incipient vomiting. Some of the women hurried to her and supported her head in their hands, whispering aloud, 'Why can't they leave the poor creature alone?'

I entirely agreed with them and murmured to myself, 'Good heavens. I'd like to leave her alone, but what am I to do? The Public Prosecutor's office is waiting for the forms and questionnaires!'

One of the women took courage and said, 'You want to know her name, sir? Her name is Nabawiya.'

'Nabawiya what?'

'Nabawiya — that's all we know. Whenever she comes along the street, we say, "Come along, Nabawiya; do this, Nabawiya; do that Nabawiya!"'

But this was quite inadequate; it was essential to write her name in full, so I implored the women to help me make her speak for a second. They thronged round her and lifted her head, which was slumped on her chest, and whispered in her ear, requesting her to speak and answer the Legal Officer. A full hour passed before she moved her lips, whereat the women took heart and slapped her shoulders encouragingly: 'Yes, yes — answer us, dearie!'

I hastily shouted into her ear, 'Your name! What's your name?' I was dripping with perspiration.

'Oh... my name? Nabawiya!'

I could have torn my clothes in exasperation. 'Yes, I know, I know! That's fine. But — Nabawiya what? What's your father's name? It's your father's name I want. Nabawiya what?'

But it was like addressing a corpse. Her head collapsed and slumped back on her chest. She was silent but for a low groan. I was overcome with annoyance and despair and shouted resoundingly at the women. They hurriedly raised her head again and sprinkled her temples with cold water and cajoled her gently, until we finally obtained her full name.

117

There remained ten items in the questionnaire. If the name itself required all this effort, what of the rest? Especially the last question — about the period which elapsed between when the suspicious substance was administered and when the first symptoms appeared, duly mentioning all the dates clearly and the exact time, as the 'Note' demanded. This woman who had not uttered her name until we were nearly dead with exhaustion was supposed to tell us the exact hour and minute when she first noticed the symptoms. I should be mad to put such questions; it would be simply obtuse. What would these women think of my intelligence when they saw me vigorously preoccupied in obtaining from this woman — who lay there like a corpse — all kinds of details about the hour and minute of her symptoms and all the rest of the printed formulas which had been drawn up with calm deliberation in the capital, far from the scene of her squalid anguish?

I made a sign to the clerk to close his Report and indicated that the victim could not be interrogated. We contented ourselves with taking specimens of the excrement and cutting off the suspected assailant's nails and pockets. We then returned to the Legal Department, where I threw myself, exhausted, into a chair.

I closed my eyes for a while and then opened them at the sound of a door being opened. My assistant came in. He was as pale as a ghost. I awoke from my torpor and began to question him. 'What's the matter with you?'

'It's the post mortem.'

'Oh, you were there while it was being done? What was the result?'

'The result is that I... I...'

He sat on a chair next to me. I stared at him intently and all became clear. He had undergone the same experience as I had when I first attended a post mortem examination. He was a sensitive young man who had just left his books; the very books which demonstrated that man is a magnificent

creature, the axis of the universe, the being chosen above all others for the Creator's provident care, a thing of light and spirit destined to be reborn. Very few people had ever been vouchsafed an opportunity of seeing the composition of this creature from within. Anyone who witnessed that sight would experience a shock which he would interpret in his own way, according to his temperament and upbringing.

I shall never forget the day when I stood for the first time at the head of a corpse whose brain had been pierced by a bullet from close range, which had broken the skull and torn the right auricular wall, so that some of the brain substance protruded. The doctor came to carry out the autopsy and I went with him to see what he would do. We left the field in which the murder took place and went to the victim's house — a modest country cottage. The murdered man was carried in by his family, who had wrapped him in a brand new sheet, surrounded by women wailing, shrieking and befouling their faces with mud. The energetic ma'mur who was with us ordered his men to clear the place of all spectators except the police, the doctor, the village barber and his assistants. Two large basins were brought in and placed under a broad wooden stretcher in the middle of the room. The barber and his assistants put the body on this stretcher and took off the dead man's clothes, which were brand new, in honour of the Great Feast. For the crime had taken place on the last day of Ramadan, as though the murderer had been fearful of allowing the feast to commence while his rival yet lived and was eager to present him with a bullet in the head as a seasonal gift, transforming the festive tones and songs which rose from within the house. The doctor passed the scalpel over the dead man's head and dictated to the clerk, 'Scalp removed.'

At this we heard the shrieks of the women, who had sneaked in over the roof of the house and neighbouring roofs, which were thatched with twigs of cotton and maize. Amidst the confused sounds I discerned a warm high-pitched voice

119

which affected me painfully and deeply: 'Oh our father, the tree in whose shade we sheltered!'

Then another voice, equally high-pitched and warm, broke in amidst sobs and tears: 'Oh, father, and after your last meal of the fast!'

By now the skin had been removed and the doctor put his finger in the opening of the wound and explored the depth and limits of the fissure. He went on dictating: 'Bullet wound four centimetres long.'

He groped for the bullet, but without success. Taking a saw from his tool case, he began to saw the skull from the front to make an opening in the head, but was unable to penetrate its hardness. So he took up a small hammer from among his instruments and began to knock on the saw, as though he were opening a box of sardines. One of the women heard this sound and, looking through the roof, beheld this hammering on the head of the father of the family and the lord of the household. She buried her face in her hands, exclaiming, 'The name of God protect him!'

This expresson startled me and I found its effect strange. This old woman still believed that her man was there in all his human personality, just at the moment when I began to doubt it.

The scalp was removed, revealing the thin membrane which is closest to the brain itself. The doctor incised it with his scalpel and began to inspect the vicinity of the wound, dictating all the time: 'Violent haemorrhage in the cervical tissue.'

Again his fingers rummaged for the bullet, but with no success. He went on groping in the area near the wound, but found no trace of the bullet. There was no other opening from which it could have fallen out. The doctor did not despair. 'Sometimes,' he said with a smile, 'the bullet takes a strange course in the body. Why, sometimes it enters the stomach and turns up in the thigh. That's quite normal. But a bullet entering the head and emerging from the foot —

120

why that's witchcraft. I can't believe that a bullet has that power.'

Eventually he lost control of his temper and exclaimed, 'Why do all this? Let's take the brain out whole!'

With both hands he removed the contents of the skull until he had emptied it like a clean bowl. He then divided the brain into four parts, of which he gave one to each of his assistants, ordering them to look carefully for the bullet. So they began to knead this substance, which is said to be the source of all human eminence, until they had reduced it to liquid paste.

'This is the human brain,' I whispered to myself. My early fright gradually dissolved. My nerves became taut and my feelings relaxed. There awoke in me a strong curiosity to see this whole body opened for my inspection. If I had seen the brain — well, I might as well see the heart, the liver, the intestines. The man was no longer a man in my sight. He was just a great clock, stretched out before me, which I wanted to open and behold its screws and springs, its wheels and bells.

After prolonged examination, nothing was found. It was just bad luck, the doctor said; but we had to get results, come what may. Here was a murdered man — surely there must be a bullet. The doctor set to work in real earnest and some impatience, running his scalpel all over the body. I stood behind him, saying, 'Go on, cut away!' I was seized by a strange fever in which I had lost all human perception. I began to talk to the doctor: 'Show me the lungs! Show me the intestines! Show me the gall-bladder...!'

The doctor did not hesitate a minute; he made an incision from the chest to the lower abdomen and took out all the organs, busily dictating: 'Heart sound. Intestines retain trace of digestion. Despite careful examination, no bullet found...'

We reflected for a moment and considered whether the bullet, being heavy, might not have fallen out of so wide a wound and dropped to the ground. We finished the operation

and departed. I was amazed by the change which had come over me. A sensitive person like myself could watch this butchery of dissection, and even instigate it — and not be afraid! And what a disillusionment it was! I had thought man to be something greater than this. No — we ought never to see ourselves from within. The image of what I had just beheld would never vanish from my mind's eye...

No doubt this same spectacle had affected my assistant. I was on the point of asking him all about it when the door opened and my servant came in with a telephone message.

'Let's hope it's good news,' I said.

I took the message, and at the first glance I emitted a sudden cry: 'The girl Rim!'

'What about her?' asked my assistant, eagerly.

'They've found her body in the canal, south of the village.'

'Dead?'

'I tell you — they've found the body. Here, read the message!'

He took the slip of paper and read it silently, until he came to the last sentence: 'Probable cause of death — asphyxiation by drowning.' His glance lingered on these words for a moment. His emotion was deep, and I was even more grieved to think that such beauty had suddenly perished.

I reflected in silence on our misfortune; not because of any professional failure or because Rim was one of the keys to the case. It was because she had been such a dazzling spectacle and had moved us all deeply — the mad and the sane amongst us alike. This sweet creature had given us some bright moments. It was as if a zephyr breeze had blown on the parched desert of our emotions in this decrepit village.

I awoke from my deep cogitation and looked up, extending my hand to my assistant to receive the message back and append the usual sentence: 'We order a post mortem.' I suddenly realized the horror of these words; I was finding them horrible for the first time in my life. We had often dissected corpses and I was quite prepared to dissect

half the population of the village. But this girl — this beauty — it seemed irreverent to cut it up to see what was inside.

The sharp eyes of my assistant discerned the text of the message. 'I suppose you intend to have a post mortem and send me along?'

'Certainly — who else is there?'

'Absolutely impossible! This morning's autopsy was quite enough. Hang it all, how can I sit around all day watching bodies being cut open? I'm an assistant Legal Officer, not an assistant undertaker. Besides, there's something special about that girl...'

I considered his excuse silently for a moment and then said, 'You're quite right. There's something special about Rim — you know, even if they gave me twenty pounds — look here, give me the message; we'll scrap the post mortem and order her to be buried, and that's the end of it.'

We had the power to take this course without exposing ourselves to censure. For the doctor who had examined the body after it was dragged from the river had decided that death was due to drowning, so that he could not have found any suspicious signs pointing to foul play. To carry out a post mortem in these circumstances would be unjustifiably pedantic. These legal draftsmen and jurists have a sort of vested interest; they always manage to behave in a reasonable, logical way. I took the pen to erase my previous order and suddenly heard a shout on the road. We rushed to the window, where we saw Shaikh Asfur running bare-headed along the road with his green stick, pursued by boys and youths and a crowd of villagers. He was yelling like a man possessed:

> Her eyelids now peruse the stream:
> The first a cod, the next a bream,
> The third beguiled her like a dream
> And drowned her...

He repeated this doggerel again and again with alternate moans and shouts, sometimes gesticulating like a preacher, as he leaped and jumped and ran to and fro until he disappeared from sight. We lingered at the window in rapt attention and then went back inside, muttering, 'Poor fellow!'

I returned to the message and took up the pen again; but doubts and anxieties welled within me. 'I heard him say she was drowned. But who drowned her?'

'Just a madman's hallucination,' said my assistant. 'We can't open an inquiry on the strength of a lunatic's chatter in the street. The best thing is to bury the girl and be done with it.'

His words banished my hesitation. I pressed firmly and resolutely on the pen as I scribbled a burial order. 'You're quite right,' I said. 'I've had enough of this case and of all concerned in it.'

22 October

I awoke late this morning, having sat up far into the night getting rid of back papers, for the new judicial year begins next week. That means I must not leave a single uncompleted case over from the outgoing year. In other words, I have to lock myself up for the whole week examining the files of complaints which fill my cupboard to overflowing. How I hate these complaints! They are more numerous than the armies of bugs which creep over the damp, tumbledown wall of our office. And they only seem to come pouring down on me on market-days. It would appear that the ordinary peasant goes off to the market every Thursday to sell his jar of maize, buy a little tea and sugar and fill his bottle with oil — and then hires one of the public letter-writers to draw up a 'statement' or 'petition' against the village squire or umdah or the assistant to the chief ghafir.

It seems to be a permanent item in the budget of every peasant who goes to the market. I cannot think why it is. Can it really be a sense of grievance, or is it just that the infection of complaint has been lodged in the fellahin's hearts throughout all the generations of oppression? In any case, I hardly deserved to absorb all the frivolity of these papers. Anyone would think that a Legal Officer did not have enough to do in attending court sessions and recording charges in the morning, drafting misdemeanours and felonies in the evening, and going out on investigations in the middle of the night. All this was not enough, and the Legal Officer was still supposed to have time to breathe — so one might as well smother him with sheaves of trivial papers from the police station called 'Complaints' or 'Petitions' or 'Situation Reports'. With my poor physique and frail constitution, and my sensitive temperament which found such pleasure in a half an hour alone with a good book, I still had to read about the exchange of abuse between Sitt al-Dar and her neighbour Kataif; about the notices of lost signet-rings received by the police; and situation reports about a donkey which had run away from outside a house; about a child who had cut his foot by treading on a piece of glass, and about a sycamore branch which fell on the head of Haj Habbab's goat! I really have great sympathy for a certain Legal Officer in Upper Egypt who is said to have crossed the Nile in a boat in order to reach his headquarters. He was carrying a load of those complaints and did not know what to do; so he made a sign to the boatman, who turned the craft over on its side and sent the 'complaints' into the water!

My plight is made much worse by Abd al-Maqsud Effendi, the Head of the Criminal Section, whose duty it is to send the case-lists at the proper time to the Public Prosecutor and the Minister of Justice. This man seems to have nothing to do except to wander from one room to another with a paper containing orders to do this, and not to do that. He has even transferred the duty of executing judgments to some of his

subordinates while he contents himself with the task of shouting at the clerks and attendants. He is always the first official to go home. He has a way of fixing his gold-rimmed spectacles on his nose and glaring at the advocates and litigants assembled in the corridors of the Legal Department, as though exhorting them to rise in his honour. His conversation is limited to a recitation of his close contacts and acquaintances with senior officials, which he recounts with inordinate pride. I have often asked him for an account of his work, and he invariably replies, 'Thank God, I'm not a fellow inclined to boasting and swank.'

That is hardly an answer to my question. It seems that some people often utter words in their defence which themselves imply a frank accusation. *Qui s'excuse s'accuse.* In a way, every defendant wraps up evidence of his guilt in the very folds of his speech, just as the sick man carries the germs of disease in his blood.

So I was condemned to exhausting work in order to close the judicial year properly. I ordered my door to be shut, so that I could be alone with the files and distribute them left and right, as their contents demanded. 'If you take something from the pile, it decreases,' I said to myself as I toiled away; but the author of that saying must have been thinking in terms of piles of gold. The piles of complaint forms were an ever-increasing quantity, never diminishing or dwindling away. Will man ever cease from complaining, as long as he breathes on earth?

I lost myself in my work and did not hear a light knock at the door. I suddenly saw a well-dressed man in the middle of my room smiling at me; a servant stood behind him with two suitcases. This was a strange visit; it was none other than the Legal Officer from Tanta. What on earth had brought him here? And what were these suitcases for? My colleague gave me no time to speculate; he ordered his servant to put the suitcases down and depart. As soon as we were alone, he threw himself on his knees in a theatrical attitude:

126

'I have fallen from heaven and you have received me!' he exclaimed.

I looked at his corpulent frame and my slender hands. 'What's that? I've received you? Are you crazy or what?'

'Listen. It's a serious matter. You're well known to all of us as a zealous, generous…'

I began to smell a rat: it was plain that my colleague had left his office in Tanta at a delicate time — the anniversary of the Sayyid al-Badawi, which was always an occasion for crowding the city with throngs of pilgrims. The result was always a glut of incidents and disturbances, as at every anniversary and every occasion when crowds gathered. He had obviously left all that behind and had recourse to my 'zeal' and 'generosity' for asking a big favour. What sort of favour could it be? I was besieged by anxieties and wanted to know his request immediately, so that I could be relieved of suspense.

'I'm at your service,' I said.

As soon as he heard these words of encouragement, he rushed at me and began kissing my head, prattling away like a street beggar: 'God preserve you. God prolong your life…'

He then left me abruptly and threw himself on the suitcases. 'Will you excuse me a moment?' he said.

'Good heavens,' I replied, inwardly admiring his good taste and courtesy, 'you shouldn't have bothered to bring a present, you know.'

He opened one of the suitcases; I expected the first one to contain at the very least some of the seasonal chickpeas with which the anniversary of Sayyid al-Badawi is associated and the second one to be full of the traditional cakes. Instead, he produced loads of complaints and put them on my table. 'A humble gift, according to my means,' he said modestly.

'Heaven help me!' I mumbled, staring at the papers.

My guest went on producing files in endless succession. 'Even the Prophet accepted presents,' he said.

I found no words for this creature who persisted in calling

this imposition a 'present'. I cursed the familiar motto that 'The Legal Department knows no barriers.' This was our guiding principle, which required mutual co-operation between all members of the department and gave the Legal Officer in Aswan the right to deal with the cases of his colleague in Alexandria in complete disregard of all considerations of time and place. I cursed the system, my guest and myself; it was indeed a misfortune that I had a reputation amongst my colleagues for being an efficient worker — especially in dealing rapidly with formal complaints. Many of my fellow Legal Officers had adopted my method in reading these petitions; they used to say that I read a complaint from the end to the beginning, which is quite true. I'm not so stupid as to read those papers from the beginning like ordinary sane people; if I did that, I would never finish reading. What I do is to glance at the preamble with all its fine phrases such as 'Oh, Refuge of Justice, Champion of the Right, Destroyer of the Rule of Oppression, etc, etc'. I then look at the last line, which usually contains the heart of the matter; even this essence is not entirely essential, and my pen runs through it, writing the words 'file for reference', with a rapid zeal and audacity which excite the envy of my colleagues, as they flounder helplessly in oceans of nonsense.

Today, however, I was the last person to assist anybody else; in fact, I was in sore need of help myself. The descent of this guest was sheer misfortune and a most grievous blow. I could not disguise my feelings and grimaced sadly as the petitions came pouring out of the suitcases.

'That's fine, that's very fine,' I said, in ironical rage. 'Look at these anniversary dainties! It's enough to break your heart!'

My visitor disposed of the last veil: 'Actually, I meant to bring you some cakes and...'

'Not of this kind, I hope!' I replied in terror.

He went on with a smile: 'But it clean slipped out of my mind at the last moment!'

'Thank God for that!'

My respected colleague laughed. Coffee was brought in and he drank it with the usual salutation. He then got up and walked round the room, going up to the window in his usual way and surveying the scattered houses on either side. 'There's a pretty girl in that house,' he said, winking slyly.

'I thought you'd learnt sense and stopped making a fool of yourself,' I said, pulling him firmly by the arm.

He laughed as he came back to the room and resumed his seat. 'What do you mean — making a fool of myself? Flirting — why, it's in my blood!'

He proceeded to remind me of our days in Deirut, when we used to work together in the Legal Department. He then demanded a cigarette and began to smoke it, saying, 'Do you remember at Deirut — how we used to stand at the window looking over the roofs for a woman's chemise worked in lace — just to convince ourselves that women really existed in those parts?'

That country was indeed primitive and barbarous. The southern part of Egypt is terrifying for the inhabitants of the Delta: women there are like invisible phantoms, not meet to be seen; and they are withered creatures, hardly different from men. Both sexes had no vestige of gentleness. In body, nature and spirit they both resembled the dark soil on which they lived — soil dried by the ebb of the Nile during the subsiding of the water. These people, too, were left dry in their characters when the waters of human personality ebbed away.

He puffed smoke from his nose and mouth and continued: 'God confound that place! I bet that if you opened the heads of nine-tenths of the people of Deirut, you'd find them shaken up through being whacked with steel piping.'

I nodded assent. 'And what about Abnub?' I said.

'Damn Abnub!'

He accompanied the curse with a gesture which made me smile. I was reminded of something I had read about that

village. It appears that statistics had been published in Europe or America — I can't remember which — to clarify the position of crime all over the world. It was stated that Chicago came first amongst the cities of the world in abundance of crime and was closely followed by Abnub! The other famous cities of the world came later on the list. At the time I would have thought that Abnub was a city in America — but for a footnote in the margin stating that it was a place in Upper Egypt. I was astonished to find that little town possessing such prestige amongst the world's famous cities — even though it was a dubious status in the sphere of crime. Chicago and Abnub — the two poles of humanity's baser instincts! The first exemplified the crime of civilization; the latter — the crime of the desert. And each of them had its own nature and characteristics.

The crime of civilized society assumed a civilized garb in respect of its weapons, its objects and its motives. It went out in armour-plated cars with revolvers and machine-guns and explosives to attack massive banks and stores, and subsequently returned to its hiding place with great hoards of money. Primitive crime, on the other hand, sallied forth skulking behind the folds of long robes, carrying an axe or hammer or shotgun to shed the blood of some insignificant victim in revenge for some slight offence in accordance with traditional customs. On the one side — money; on the other — hallowed traditions. Such is the difference between civilized and primitive society, between the preoccupation of civilized man and the concerns of backward people. Evil is always evil, but surely evil arising from some great cause is more worthy of respect than evil springing from some absurd triviality. A high degree of civilization may not do away with evil or abolish crime, but at least it produces evil and crime in the grand manner.

I turned to my silent colleague and addressed him: 'I'm absolutely fed up! I'm tired of the provinces! I'm utterly sick of peasants' HATS!'

'You can be as fed up as you like.'

'I'm just longing for Cairo! I've forgotten what my own capital looks like. I want a different sort of crime. I want criminals in jackets and trousers!'

'There are postings and transfers in November.'

'I think it's my turn to be posted to Cairo.'

'Cairo postings don't come in turns, old man. Have you any influence?'

'None.'

'Then you'll live and die in the provinces.'

'And what about our colleagues who have been sitting in Cairo taking it easy for years?'

'The transfers will affect them, too, but in the usual way and the time-honoured method. The Legal Officer of the Muski will be transferred to the Ezbekieh office. The Legal Officer of Shubra will be moved to Khalifa. The Legal Officer of Sayyidah Zainab will be moved to the University area. In other words, transfers which involve no departure from the metropolitan paradise. And for all that, our honourable friends won't be satisfied. One of them will say, "Shubra — Good Lord — Shubra is frightfully far from my house in Zamalek." Another one will say, "How on earth can I go to the Sayyidah Zainab office? It's such a low neighbourhood!" As for you and me — you'll be sent to Fechn — God forbid! — and I'll be packed off from Tanta to Tama or Manfalut. And if either of us mutters a word of complaint or dissatisfaction, they'll hurl abuse at us and say, "Who are these pampered fellows, anyway? Go off to your posts and don't make a fuss!"'

I kept quiet, absorbed in bitterness and rancour, finding no better course than to be patient so as not to add to the general misfortune. 'We're in God's hands,' I said with a sigh. 'God is with us. Still — it's enough to put anyone off his work...' As I spoke, my glance fell on the piles of papers which I had to deal with and I felt my zeal for work turning to apathy.

131

'Work, work,' said my colleague. 'Why, that's the last thing to interest our great big chiefs. Influence first, and the public welfare last. Whether you're amenable or antagonistic to work is a question which none of our great chiefs understands or is interested in.'

He looked at his watch and jumped up, bidding me farewell: but I held on to him like grim death, for it was a relief and consolation to have his company and exchange reminiscences. 'Sit down. you must lunch with me today.'

'Sorry, I can't. My office is empty and it's the time of the festival. Please excuse me...'

He thanked me and held out his hand with a rapid goodbye. He pointed to the files of complaints which he had brought along with him. 'I hope you're in good fettle for the pile of papers I presented you with. Next time I'll have some sweets for you — I really will — chickpeas, sesame, nuts, almonds, pistachio...'

'All right; go away now! My mouth is watering in anticipation.'

I saw him off to the door with a smile and he vanished from sight. I went back to my work but I was bored, dispirited and sick at heart. I glanced at the complaints again and decided to carry on with my work without wasting time in useless recrimination, which would be quite unnoticed except by the four walls which held my spirit in captivity. I took up my pen, seized the first file and read, 'Oh Refuge of Justice...' I burst into loud, unrestrained laughter. Fancy — me the Refuge of Justice! Where was Justice? I don't know it and have never set eyes on it, since nobody has ever shown it to me. They expect me to attend to other people's complaints and never deign to pay heed to my complaints and those of all my colleagues. I scribbled 'File for reference' lavishly over most of the papers. Abd al-Maqsud Effendi entered with some thick files.

'What's all this?' I said in a tone of panic.

'Cases remaining to be dealt with. These are the mis-

demeanours. Boy, bring the felony cases!' he added with a yell behind him. He looked at me and asked, 'What shall I do with the other felonies?'

He put some files before me. On the uppermost file-cover I read, 'Case of Kamar al-Dawla Alwan'. I remembered that the culprit had naturally not been discovered — and never would be discovered. How could we be expected to find the culprit in an obscure case like this, when the ma'mur and all his policemen were buried up to their heads in falsifying the election results, while I was overwhelmed with reading complaints and misdemeanours and contraventions and in attending court? If only we had some secret police in the modern fashion, and an investigating magistrate who would concentrate wholly on crime cases, as in Europe and the civilized world! There they take people's lives seriously, whereas here nobody does. Money is spent on the most trivial affairs but, if you ask for some for the purpose of establishing justice or improving the condition of the people, it becomes scarce and meagre, gripped by trembling hands, as though one was about to throw it into the sea. The reason is that 'justice' and 'the people' are words whose significance is still unknown in this country. They are just phrases whose only purpose is to be written on paper and delivered in orations, like many other words and moral attributes whose existence is not tangibly felt. So why should I be expected to take the life of Mr Kamar al-Dawla seriously? The poor wretch had died and been finished with — like hundreds of similar victims in this and other districts. Their blood had been shed more cheaply than the ink with which their case reports were inscribed; and their memory had been officially erased with the final simple formula: 'Case filed for reference owing to non-discovery of assailant. Inform police and continue investigation.' The police then replies in a familiar sentence known by heart, which the orderly clerk types out as he munches a carrot: 'Am continuing investigation.' This is a valedictory phrase wherewith the case is finally buried.

And yet the case of Kamar al-Dawla had been illumined by a radiance which distinguished it in our eyes from other cases and imparted zest to our laborious efforts on its behalf. Now this radiance had departed for ever, and the special character of the episode was forgotten: it had become a case like scores of others whose personal aspects had no interest for us at all. And yet such a case, or rather such a file of papers, had a specific personality in the eyes of legal people. The highest quarters of the law were interested in the file and the speed of its disposal, and did not blame us at all for having the case filed for reference. They would have blamed us heartily if we allowed the case to remain under investigation and to be entered accordingly in the list sent to the Public Prosecutor and the ministry at the end of the judicial year. What a disgrace that would be, and what heinous neglect would be attributed to the Legal Officer! What a mass of urgent correspondence would descend upon his head from all sides if the case remained under active consideration! If he replied that he had not exhausted his inquiries or arrived at the discovery of the criminal and was persistently continuing his investigation, the excuse would not be accepted. His colleagues would think him a fool and regard him as a novice. Their advice would be to file the case 'provisionally', so that it would be considered as having been dealt with. For higher quarters were concerned and satisfied only by dealing with cases, which meant washing one's hands of them and getting free of them somehow, so that they could record them in their statistical record: 'This year x cases of felony were recorded in this area and y cases were dealt with, etc, etc.' The greater the number of cases dealt with, the more conclusive the evidence of zeal on the part of the legal staff and others in preserving good order and assisting the smooth working of the administrative machine.

Abd al-Maqsud Effendi pointed to the files and said, 'First of all, sir, deal with the pile of outstanding felony cases, so

that I can close the list and send it to his excellency the Public Prosecutor and the ministry.'

'What — just like that? All right!'

I dipped the pen in the ink and took up the first case — Kamar al-Dawla Alwan. 'If you want me to deal with it — I'll deal with it.'

I wrote the stereotyped formula at the foot of the Report: 'Case filed and held over owing to non-discovery of assailant, etc, etc.'

I then pulled out the other cases and did exactly the same. As I handed the file to the Head of the Criminal Section, I said to him, 'Now are you satisfied? We've finished. The case list is complete!'

Despite myself, a tone of bitter mockery was in my voice.